DEAR ABBY

ON

PLANNING

YOUR

WEDDING

Dear Abby
ON
PLANNING YOUR
Wedding

By

ABIGAIL VAN BUREN

Andrews and McMeel

A Universal Press Syndicate Company

Kansas City • New York

Design by Barrie Maguire

Grateful acknowledgment is made to the following for granting permission to reprint copyrighted material:

The essay by Carolyn R. Flint originally appeared in the *Hartford Courant,* copyright © 1988 by Carolyn R. Flint

The essay by Chris Thomas originally appeared in the *Dallas Morning News,* copyright © 1988 by the *Dallas Morning News*

Library of Congress Cataloging in Publication Data
Van Buren, Abigail
    Dear Abby on planning your wedding / by Abigail van Buren.
      p. cm.
    ISBN 0-8362-7943-3 : $8.95
     1. Wedding etiquette—United States. 2. Weddings—United States.
    I. Title.
    BJ2051.V35 1989
    395'.22—dc19

                                     88-31224
                                         CIP

Contents

for you!

Introduction

Every day I receive thousands of letters about love. Among them are humorous stories, tales of anguish, complaints, and questions about that enduring symbol of love: the wedding.

Whether you are the bride-to-be or the grandmother of the groom, many of you are confused about weddings. And I can see why. Here's a sample of the dilemmas that face contemporary couples of all ages:

"What's traditional and what isn't if my parents and my new in-laws have all been divorced and remarried? Who gets photographed with whom? Who should stand in the receiving line? Should my fiancé and I just give up and elope?"

"What should I wear if this is my second time around? I really look terrific in black and I can't afford a new dress."

"I'm Jewish and she's Japanese. What kind of ceremony are we supposed to have?"

I'm sure you get the picture. Add to this confusion the fact that suddenly the marriage picture has changed. Thousands of people are choosing to marry after putting the idea on hold for so many years.

Yet another surprise is that over 30 percent of the 2.5 million marriages annually are *second,* even third, trips to the altar. Altar? That's changed, too. I heard from one bride who wanted to be married in a hot-air balloon!

Consider, too, all the mixed messages we get from magazines, television, and newspapers. The retailers are romancing potential brides and grooms with so many new products and services that we are looking at weeks—months of exhausting research and planning.

The event that should be one of the most joyful and memorable of our lives suddenly begins to look like an endless project. Often, the final straw is tradition.

Tradition? Talk about old history. People are no longer adhering to the old traditions, particularly when it come to "The Wedding." For example:

• There are couples who both work and don't have the time to plan an old-fashioned wedding extravaganza—and may well feel that the money could be better spent elsewhere.

• Many of us live so far from our families that travel becomes a major expense—especially if the families live on different coasts.

• Some of you have special circumstances such as a marriage ceremony that you want to be comfortable, not only for yourselves as bride and groom, but also for your children, soon-to-be-step-children, and all your friends who need to know how to handle the new, *blended* family.

How can you resolve all these questions and still have a wonderful day? Are there easy solutions?

Believe it or not, there are. In these pages I've collected the wisdom of many. From my own experience as a mother and grandmother, from the advice of my experts, and, most important, from the experiences of my readers, I have culled the best "how-to's" and easy-to-follow guidelines.

As I share with you the experiences of my readers—you are sure to learn something that will make your wedding more "special."

In my years as an advice columnist, I've learned that there is not just *one* way to do things. That's why I feel it's important that you acquaint yourself with "new options"—dealing with lovers who marry in ways other than the traditional, choosing styles that reflect their own personalities. Dare to be different!

You, too, can have a wonderful wedding—doing it *your* way and knowing that it will be *right*!

How New Traditions Are Replacing the Old

A couple that fits the profile of many young people today: They both work, they are in their late twenties, their resources are limited—but they want to have a big wedding with all the trimmings:

Dear Abby: My fiancé and I are financially independent of our folks and we just don't make that much money yet. Both of us have cars to pay for, clothes to buy, and we need to rent a bigger place. So, even though we want to have a big wedding, we just can't afford it! What can we do?

Betrothed but Betwixt

Dear B and B: Some of the best things in life are free. Take a lesson from a couple who tied the knot with a very short shoestring. Their maid-of-honor wrote to tell me about it:

Dear Abby: Anne and Bill had $1,500 to spend for their wedding and honeymoon. They set aside money for the honeymoon, leaving $960 for everything else. They discussed their dilemma with their closest friends because they wanted to invite about two hundred guests but they couldn't afford it. The corner-cutting solutions their friends provided a wedding as memorable as money could buy. Read on:

Instead of a formal reception, Anne and Bill asked their minister if they could use the church basement immediately following the ceremony. The minister was happy to oblige thinking this would encourage other couples to use the church and help defray utility bills.

Friends helped the couple set up tables and cover them with white butcher paper. The same friends announced that their wedding gifts would be overflowing pots of wildflowers they would pick themselves to decorate the "reception hall." Other friends made a list of refreshments, and everyone brought a dish. Instead of champagne, the bride and groom served sparkling cider, which *everyone* enjoyed—including the children!

The ten attendants chose to either make their own bridesmaids' dresses or rent their own tuxedos as their individual wedding gifts. The bride wore her mother's wedding gown. When she discovered the high cost of a veil, she shortened the dress and used the extra fabric to make silk flowers for a "tiara" to which she attached a few yards of tulle. Her hairdresser's wedding gift was a complimentary hairdo!

Suddenly, almost the entire wedding was free, and the bride could spend her dollars on a special wedding cake. She had saved a picture from a magazine years before which she took to the local bakery, hoping she could afford something on the order of the beautiful eight-tier cake. They made exactly what she had always dreamed of having!

So everyone came, had a wonderful time—and all on a shoestring budget.

The following chapters have been carefully organized to lead you through planning your own wedding.

I will describe the traditional as well as the untraditional, and you may decide what is right for you. I'll advise you on such matters as the type of ceremony, the proper seating arrangement at the rehearsal dinner, and cutting the wedding cake.

Each chapter includes basic instructions and checklists that detail every element you should consider—with space provided to record your decisions. At the back of the book are deadline guides for the bride and the groom plus a section for organizing your final month. It can all be tucked into your purse, making it easy for you to be on top of each and every detail.

Dear Abby on Planning Your Wedding will not only save you time, it will be a keepsake in years to come as you recall the wonderful memories of your special day.

Will you do me one favor as you use this guide? Please make detailed notes, and if your wedding turns out to be as extraordinary as I think it will, write and tell me about it for my next edition.

Thank you, and . . . best wishes!

Dear Abby

Please write to me at this address:

Dear Abby
P.O. Box 69440
Los Angeles, California 90069

Or, address your letter to:

Dear Abby
c/o Your Local Newspaper

1

"Great Expectations"

Q: Dear Abby,
What makes a wedding perfect?

A: Knowing what to expect, and how to make it all come true.

Don't be deceived by the easy answer. If you were to read my mail, you'd be amazed by how the number of brides who say that a perfect wedding is an impossible dream!

One bride has a fairy-tale image that doesn't quite fit her pocketbook, while another breezes merrily along, planning the special day, only to discover it's not exactly what her fiancé had in mind.

So let's back up a bit and define "the perfect wedding."

I think it's one that is everything the bride and groom want it to be—with the understanding that they take time to explore not only what they want but *how to get it*.

Keep in mind that getting there is half the fun. Then spelling out your "great expectations" becomes part of the joy of getting married. It's not as easy as it used to be.

Why? Because over the last two decades three major social changes have occurred that not only affect your life, but have changed the way you plan your wedding.

First, men and women marry at an older age today. They still fall in love in their teens, but they wisely choose to wait until their careers are established before they "take the veil."

Many are marrying in their mid- to late twenties rather than immediately upon graduation from high school or college. This means the bride and the groom are likely to be more involved in the "planning *and paying*" stages of a wedding than couples were in the past. No longer is the bride's family expected to shoulder the full financial burden. (Hooray—it's about time!)

Second, because most brides and grooms work and see themselves as "equal partners," yet another social phenomenon is occurring. Many grooms expect to be more involved in planning the wedding.

Today's groom has no intention of sitting on the sidelines while one of the most significant events of his life is being planned.

And finally—but just as critical—is the impact that divorce has on weddings. I can tell you that confusion reigns as brides and grooms try to stage happy events involving all the parents, grandparents, step-parents and other "blended family" members, without hurting anyone's feelings.

Some couples are marrying for the second or third time, which puts a new spin on old traditions.

Fulfilling great expectations also means planning the details of your wedding to consider any previous marriages and divorces that may have taken place in your families.

The flawless wedding is possible all right. But it "happens" when the bridal couple knows how to mix practical detail with the emotional insights and special kindnesses that make their wedding memorable for its warmth.

Sound like a challenge? It is—but it will require careful planning. And where better to begin than with a short list of what to avoid.

Honest Errors Committed by Most Brides and Grooms

Honest Error Number One—The Forgotten Father

Oh Dad, poor Dad. And I'm not talking about leaving him at the airport.

This is the guy who wants the best for everyone, whether he's the father of the bride or the groom, yet he is often the last to be asked about *his* expectations for this wonderful event.

Only after the plans have been laid is he included—and then it's usually to pick up the tab.

Put Dad at the top of the list of people to be consulted from the very beginning. I'm told that one bride's father's contribution to the wedding was, "Just get married by the end of the year so you can file joint tax returns!" Good advice!

Here's one fellow who never should have had to write me a letter—but maybe his words will save the day for dads everywhere:

> Dear Abby: Our family is approaching a time of dissension concerning the upcoming wedding of our eldest daughter. Recent weddings of friends and family have been real "blowouts," each trying to outdo the last.
>
> My wife and daughters keep talking about the reception, gowns, flowers, and tuxedos as if we had a perennial money tree. They justify a "nice" wedding for the "memories" it will make.
>
> I believe that a "nice" wedding can consist of a bride's gown, and simple dresses for the ladies that won't cost them a fortune—preferably one they can wear again. And what's wrong with dark blue suits for the men, and cake and punch for the reception?
>
> We aren't rich, but we meet our needs and have no bad debt problems—yet! My wife uses coupons to shop at the grocery store and she manages our money matters very well, but no amount of coupons will be able to cover the disaster they are planning. What do you say?
>
> Has the Ladder Set Up

> Dear Has: Take down the ladder, I'm on your side. A wedding need not be an extravaganza to be memorable, nor does it have to top a previous one. Hold that line, and don't let your family talk you into going into debt to put on a show you can't afford.

So, you mothers and daughters and sons, check out Dad's opinion. He loves you and wants the best, but a wedding that strains the budget will be a joy to no one.

A special word to modern brides: If you are one of those bright, hardworking young women who earns five times what your father did at your age, don't be surprised if he expects you to help pay for your lovely wedding.

Better yet, why don't you *offer,* and ask Dad to help you with the budget? And if the groom's family can afford to pitch in, and they offer, then by all means, allow them to—graciously.

Honest Error Number Two—The Misunderstood Mom

Today's mother of the bride is put in the most bewildering position. Where once she was the guardian of family traditions, wedding and otherwise, now she's likely to find herself at the mercy of new social situations that lead to confusion.

Dear Abby: My mother is ruining my wedding plans. I left my hometown four years ago to work in a city two hundred miles away, and this is where I want to get married. My fiancé is from this city and so are my friends and his. We're planning to get married in his church here, but my mother says if I don't get married in my hometown in the church she attends, she won't come to my wedding. She accuses me of wanting to get married here to hurt her, and says if I loved her, I'd get married in her church. I do love her, but she makes me feel so guilty.

I can't talk to my father about this because he always agrees with Mother to avoid an argument. I've talked to my priest, who agrees that the problem is my mother, but he has offered no solution.

My fiancé's parents have tried to get Mother to change her mind, but it's no use. Who's wrong? My mother or me?

The Something Blue Is Me

Dear Blue: I can understand why your mother would rather have your wedding in her church. In her day, she would have been right. But now, in your day, I think she is wrong to refuse to attend unless you do as she wishes.

Today, with so many young women establishing their careers—and friendships—in cities far from home, it is not unusual for the wedding to take place in one location and small "receptions" be given at a later date in the hometowns of the bride and groom. It is quite proper for an invitation to the later reception to be included in your wedding invitation, if you wish.

To all mothers of modern brides: I understand the dilemma you face as you try to help with a wedding for a daughter who (a) may live far from you; (b) may already be living with the man she plans to marry, (c) may be marrying for the second or third time; and (d) may be undecided about *your* role as she herself is planning to pay for part (or all) of her wedding.

The important thing to remember about that "dilemma" is this: It signals that a new solution is just around the corner. Believe me, nothing is seen more often in today's weddings than new solutions. So settle in with your daughter and study the options together.

However, it's just as important that your daughter and her fiancé be aware of *your* new role today. You may be a working mom with little time for planning and executing all the details. You may be a single parent with less money to spend. And you may be involved in a new romance of your own.

One thing is definite. You will be experiencing many mixed emotions during these weeks and months before the wedding. Your daughter's marriage means "letting go" in a way that will change your relationship forever.

Since most grooms are becoming more involved in wedding plans, you may find that his mother is interested in putting her oars in the water, too. Be alert to the emotional effect this might have.

And if you are the mother of the groom—congratulations and good luck. You may want to have a heart-to-heart with the bride's mother as I'm sure you share many hopes and concerns.

I dedicate the following letter to moms. I just hope it was answered in time:

Dear Abby: I'm engaged to marry a wonderful man. We're both twenty-two. His mother and I get along fantastically. I call her "Mom." She says that I am the "daughter" she's always wanted but never had.

Mom asked me if she could come along with my mother and me and help pick out my bridal gown. Seeing no reason why she shouldn't, I told her I'd love to have her.

Well, I told my mother, and she said she thought it was totally rude of my future mother-in-law to include herself. Then she said if "Mom" wants to help pick out my wedding gown, she should pay for half of it!

Abby, I've already told "Mom" she could come along, and it would break her heart if I had to tell her I changed my mind. How should this be handled without making my own mother look bad?

In the Middle

Dear In: Tell you mother that you've made your future mother-in-law welcome, and there is no way you can exclude her now without causing hard feelings.

Be patient with your mother. She could be jealous of the woman with whom she must now share her daughter. Tell your mother that you want yours to be a happy, lasting marriage, and one of the most essential ingredients is a loving relationship with your husband's mother.

11

Honest Error Number Three—Short Shrift for the In-Laws

This can happen easily—forgetting to include the groom's parents as ideas are tossed around in the early stages of planning.

It happens for many reasons: They live far away, some families do not communicate as easily with their sons as with daughters, some couples forget that the old-fashioned tradition of the groom's family playing a small role in the wedding is no longer the rule.

Whenever there's a little interfamily tension, remember that grooms are such wonderful guys because they were raised by terrific parents.

Be sure to take time to consider the expectations of these "terrific parents" as wedding plans fall into place.

"Mad in Massachusetts"—whom you will meet in a moment—offers a clear picture of all that can go awry when communication with in-laws gets off to a bad start:

Dear Abby: Our son is getting married in September. When "Evelyn," the bride's mother, called to tell me of the wedding plans, I was floored! They are having the reception at the most expensive hall in Boston. Abby, these are young kids who have nothing!

I was informed that our share would be forty-five hundred dollars. I told Evelyn we didn't have that kind of money, that one thousand dollars was our limit. She hung up on me.

I called a few days later and asked how many guests we could invite to the reception. "For one thousand dollars," she said, "one couple." I was furious and went right to her house to talk to her. She said I was living in the Dark Ages if I thought the parents of the bride still paid for the whole wedding with no help from the groom's side. She repeated, our share was forty-five hundred dollars. I said, "People who put on showy weddings they can't afford are four-flushers." Then the father of the bride threw me out of the house!

Now there's bad feeling on both sides. Should we take out a loan?

Mad in Massachusetts

Dear Mad: No. The parents of the bride should have had a meeting with you before they planned a wedding that was beyond their means. Having committed for it, they have no right to "bill" you. If they have to get a loan, it will be their problem, not yours.

Money fights are not uncommon between "his" folks and "hers," even before the knot is tied. So be realistic, since you must share grandchildren and family celebrations in years to come.

Dear Abby: Our son is getting married, and the bride's parents are putting on a fifteen-thousand dollar wedding. According to the so-called rules of wedding etiquette, the bride's parents are supposed to foot the bill for the wedding, right?

Well, the bride's side invited between 200 and 250 guests, and are allowing us to invite only thirty! My sister just became engaged, so that adds one more. When we asked them to add one more, they asked us to drop one couple off our list. I feel like "dropping" my husband and me off our list.

We can invite only two friends from outside our family. They told us it costs one hundred dollars a couple, and my husband refuses to pay for the extras. I am furious about the limitations they have put on us. Is this fair or not?

Anonymously Yours

Dear Anon: The "rules" can be bent—and frequently are—depending upon the financial capabilities of those involved. (In some cases, the groom's family shares equally with the bride's in financing the wedding.)

There really are no hard-and-fast "rules" these days, but I think your son's future in-laws are being less than fair with you.

And the bottom line on this issue? Do as the bridal pair wishes.

Even though I am encouraging you to be aware of everyone's expectations so as not to inadvertently offend anyone—the bottom line is that the bride and groom make the decision to do it *their* way.

Of course, there's always one couple who—pardon the pun—takes the cake:

Dear Abby: I am twenty-seven and getting married in September to a wonderful young lady named Julie. She and I are nudists, as is her whole family. We have always wanted an outdoor wedding, and want to have the ceremony at the nudist camp where we met three years ago.

So far, all our invitations have been accepted—except one. You guessed it—the reluctant one is my mother. The non-nudists understand that they will not be required to be nude. My twenty-three-year-old sister and I have tried unsuccessfully to persuade Mother to attend. She refuses to budge, saying if we want her to attend, we will have to change our plans.

Shall we give her an ultimatum and stick with what we want? At this point, I feel like telling my mother we will miss her. What do you say?

Bobby in Nashville

Dear Bobby: It appears that your mother has already given you an ultimatum—either have a conventional wedding or count her out. Knowing how your mother feels about nudity, if you stick with your plans, it will clearly show her that you don't give a fig(leaf) about whether she attends or not.

P.S. Where will your best man carry the ring? I hope this covers everything.

Honest Error Number Four—The Bride's Wish Is Everyone's Command

Sorry, but reality intrudes in some matters.

The seventies and eighties may have raised our tolerance level of couples living together without marriage, but it happens to have worked both ways.

Nowhere is that made more clear than when parents are suddenly asked to fulfill a traditional parental role in what we can delicately call "a nontraditional situation."

The following may change *your* expectations:

Dear Abby: My fiancé and I have been living together for the last year. Before we lived together, my parents offered to pay the entire cost of our wedding. We are being married soon and have started to make the final arrangements, but their offer has not been mentioned again.

What is the tradition regarding who pays for the wedding? And does living together change the rules?

Curious Bride-to-Be

Dear Curious: Traditionally, the bride's parents pay for the wedding, but there are no "rules" that obligate them to do so. (It's a gift.)

Traditionally, the couple waits until after they are married to live together, so possibly your parents broke with the tradition of paying for your wedding because you and your fiancé broke with tradition by living together.

I suggest you discuss this with your parents.

14

And while we're on the subject of "bride's wishes," heaven help the woman who neglects to run the planning chart past her husband-to-be.

What if you want to polka but he wants jazz, you want it low-key and he wants pizzazz. Get the picture?

The Divorce Daze

To split or not to split—that was the question when Mom and Dad first went their separate ways.

Now it's, "Who gets to go to the wedding?" Or, "If your father is there, you can count me out!" Some feelings may never change.

Talk about the intricacies of planning a wedding—rarely is it as difficult as when your folks have been divorced. For some couples, this can be a challenge that equals orchestrating the betrothal of Princess Di and Charles.

I know how hard it can be. My mail is filled with letters from people totally confused and often hurt by the emotional fallout of divorce.

A word of caution to all future husbands and wives. Don't underestimate the problem. Even if you get 'em *all* to the church on time, who knows what may happen at the reception?

My advice is examine the damage potential first:

Dear Abby: My parents have been divorced since I was fourteen. I'm twenty now and have a good relationship with both my parents, but my mother resents my father for several things he has done to her as well as to me and my sister. I've learned to put things in the past and leave them there. I love my father as much as I love my mother, but Mother doesn't understand that. She doesn't expect me to hate my father, but she doesn't like it when I talk about the trips he takes with his new wife or anything he does, so I don't mention it.

I am engaged to be married and I want both parents to give me away. My mother wants to give me away and says if I insist that my father share in that honor, she will not attend my wedding. We had a long talk about it and I cried for two days. I then decided to let my mother give me away, but she knows I'm not happpy about it.

Have you any suggestions?

Worried Sick

Dear Worried: In such situations I urge parents to give their marrying child the gift of happiness on his or her wedding day, and put their own feelings aside. Your mother is wrong to punish you in her determination to punish your father. Since you love them equally, make it both or none—and ask a favorite relative or dear friend to "give you away."

It could be worse:

Dear Abby: The most mortifying thing happened at my sister's wedding last week. Her ex-husband showed up at the reception, got drunk, and started a fistfight with the best man, who was just trying to keep him away from the groom. All this right in front of the guests.

We're nice people. My Dad's a dentist and this was an expensive affair at our country club.

Here's my problem. I'm getting married in a couple of months and this troublemaker is a close relative of my fiancé. Everyone in his family says I must invite him even though it means putting all the wrong people together again.

I feel awful! I'm sure he'll start a fight and ruin my wedding. What can I do?

Bewildered Bride

Dear Bewildered: This is your wedding. You and your fiancé make the rules—no one else. This is one guest who has shown that he cannot behave like a civilized adult at a social gathering. You have every right to exclude him.

That's the bad news—now the good.

In fact, expect the best and that may be what you'll get. Here's a beautiful example of "the modern *blended* family" and how it can make a wedding day memorable:

Dear Abby: You recently published a letter from a woman who was upset because her stepdaughter had invited her husband's ex-wife to her bridal shower.

I laughed. Five years ago, I remarried in a church ceremony, and I did it my way. My stepson was my ring bearer, my teenage son gave me away, and my guests were all friends of ours. These friends included my ex-husband, my ex-in-laws, and my ex-husband's first wife. Also invited (and attended) were several people who had been significant people from the groom's past as well as my own. Many of the people I

16

worked with were there, and you should have seen their faces when I introduced these people around!

Abby, my ex-husband and his present wife are friends of mine now. He was at one time an important part of my life, and it seemed only proper that he should be present to share my joy. I suppose this is rather unusual, but my present husband's ex-wife gave me a beautiful bridal shower.

Life is too short for grudges.

I Did It My Way

Dear Did It: It would be ideal if all divorced persons would do it your way, but your way is the exception. Pity.

Since I responded to that letter, I've heard from many readers who said that their multifamily celebrations went smoothly.

Above all, as you begin to firm up who will be in the wedding party, who will be on the guest list, who will be in the wedding photos—don't be too hasty to judge. You may be in for some surprises.

Believe it or not, the "other woman" is not always heartless:

Dear Abby: I have been dating a man very seriously for the past year. (I'll call him Bill.) He and his wife have been divorced for four months. I had nothing to do with their breakup, but she despises me and refuses even to speak to me.

The problem is that Bill's daughter is getting married soon, and his "ex" is totally opposed to my attending the wedding. She says it's a family event, and I am not a member of the family.

I get along very well with Bill's daughter and her fiancé. I have offered to stay away from the wedding rather than cause a family conflict. However, the bride, the groom, and Bill have invited me to attend. The bride's mother says if I go, she will not.

My question to you is, should I attend the wedding under the cirmcumstances?

Bill's Girlfriend

Dear Girlfriend: Give Bill's daughter and her fiancé a wedding gift—a gift of love—by absenting yourself from their wedding.

Bill's "ex" has a lifetime of memories in raising her daughter, and even though she feels some anger and bitterness now, she is still the mother of the bride, and she, not you, should be there.

When I have given advice such as the above, I receive a bale of mail telling me that I'm wrong. Read on:

Dear Abby: I was appalled by your reader who raged against your commonsensical plea to let divorced parents stand together at their child's wedding, even though the parents have since remarried.

I should not have been appalled, for it is all too common for second wives to selfishly begrudge their husbands contact with their ex-wives and children, and to bitterly resent any show of generosity (gifts or money) to them.

When I married a divorced man whom I deeply loved, I encouraged him to visit his ex-wife and children and to be generous with them. And when his son married, I chose not to attend the wedding. I thought it was his child's special moment, and he would want his parents there together—which was all right with me. I knew who I was. I was his father's wife, and I also knew that the bonds established in every family do not simply go away because a divorce took place. I understood the feelings of children toward their divorced father, for I had previously had a husband who essentially abandoned our children because of the jealousy and selfishness of his second wife.

So many of us are walking around as emotional cripples because of horrendous experiences. Death we can't do much about—or unhappy childhoods—and for children, their parents' divorces. But we can do something about our private pettiness and jealousies. Let us pray for strength to control ourselves and not inflict unnecessary pain on others—especially children. Divorce is so common these days that anything we can do to soothe the wounds will invariably make us happier, and our society healthier.

Been There in California

What an extraordinarily kind and understanding woman!

Thus, the rules for planning a wedding with consideration for the blended family are simple:

One: The bride and groom shall decide who shall be invited.

Two: The more the merrier. If you can—"you" being every parent, stepparent, and significant other—set aside your personal grudges for that one special day, for the kids!

Take pride in the knowledge that this couple may have learned from your example, even your heartache, and their marriage will be much better for it.

Three: Accord the natural parents their place of honor.

And just in case you wonder if such thoughtfulness really does make a difference . . .

Dear Abby: I was recently married at a most beautiful wedding. My parents were divorced ten years ago, and since that time they had barely spoken a civil word to each other. They both attended my wedding, and were not only polite to each other, they were downright friendly! Abby, it was the best wedding present either of them could have given me.

Please print this in hopes that other divorced couples may see themselves and realize it's possible to put aside their hostilities and bitterness for just one day for the sake of their child. It made my wedding day perfect in every way.

New Bride

Dear Bride: Here's your letter with a message to divorced parents: "Read and heed, and you will compound the joy of a joyful occasion."

'Tween Confusion and Conflict

A final note of advice—be prepared to go to a third party for help if the two of you cannot resolve a particular issue involving your wedding. Consult your clergyperson first.

If it's a matter of etiquette, I recommend *The Amy Vanderbilt Complete Book of Etiquette,* revised and expanded by Letitia Baldridge (Doubleday). It is a detailed guide to accepted wedding procedures.

Second, choose an expert to provide a third *and final* opinion, which you both agree *ahead of time* to follow. That "expert" should be someone who knows you both well.

He or she may be a friend or a relative—but make the choice *before* you have your first argument.

Give that person one guideline: "Please make the decision that you feel best reflects both our personalities."

♥

The Great Expectations Quiz

I've designed this quiz to make every bride and groom aware of those issues most likely to worry or confuse a couple as they plan their wedding.

Decide together whom to approach first as you explore the expectations, concerns, and needs of your families and friends.

But remember, you, the bridal couple, make the final decisions. This wedding is *your* special day.

A. Expenses

Have you thought about the money available for your wedding expenses? Put a check by those most likely to contribute. Then, in the second column, check if you think they will expect to participate in the planning, too.

	Who Pays?	Who Plans?
1. The bride		
Self	_____	_____
Parent(s)	_____	_____
Stepparent(s)	_____	_____
2. The groom		
Self	_____	_____
Parent(s)	_____	_____
Stepparent(s)	_____	_____

B. " 'Tween Conflict and Confusion"

Have you thought about the following? Check when you are confident you know what their expectations are.

20

"GREAT EXPECTATIONS"

1. Bride's family—Do you need to consult them on:

   Planning   _____

   Ceremony/Reception   _____

   Members of wedding party   _____

   Guests   _____

   Role of stepparents   _____

   Other details   _____

                               _____

                               _____

                               _____

2. Groom's family—Do you need to consult them on:

   Planning   _____

   Ceremony/Reception   _____

   Members of wedding party   _____

   Guests   _____

   Role of stepparents   _____

   Other details   _____

                               _____

                               _____

                               _____

21

C. Your Wedding Profile

1. Major Players—List all those who will plan and help with most of the wedding:

_____

_____

_____

_____

_____

_____

_____

_____

2. Special Situations—List those unique characteristics of your families and friends that will require special attention.

_____

_____

_____

_____

_____

_____

3. Decision Guidelines—Agree on how you will resolve your problems. Do you have a third-party opinion you can rely on when you disagree?

_____

_____

_____

_____

_____

_____

_____

_____

_____

_____

_____

Now your expectations are realistic. You are well on your way to planning the perfect wedding. Have fun!

Love, Abby

2

Money Matters
Plus Wedding Budgets:
They All Add Up to...
Serious Business

Money matters—does it ever!

This is "the least and the most" stage of wedding planning—the least fun, and the most important.

This is where some pending nuptials self-destruct. Oh my, what you discover when you talk about money!

The first shock is *how much*. The sheer cost of the joyful occasion has been known to make strong men (and women) weep.

But an even greater shock is finding out how each of you feels about *spending* money. Here's an interesting device that will do more to enlighten you about life after marriage than any advice I might offer.

The Prenuptial Agreement

Let us not tiptoe around this little tulip. It is profoundly important and yet so seldom discussed . . . until it's too late.

Why? Because there is a commonly held attitude, a dangerous one I might add, that frequently appears in my mail. Here's a typical example:

> Dear Abby: What do you think of prenuptial agreements? It's my feeling that two people who really love each other should also trust each other, and if they need a signed document before they're married to be sure they aren't taken advantage of in case the marriage doesn't

work out, they shouldn't be getting married in the first place, right?
Nameless in Nevada

Dear Nameless: Wrong! A prenuptial agreement can save a great deal of fighting (in court), not to mention the cost of the legal battle. However, no one—neither man nor woman—should sign a prenuptial agreement without the advice of an attorney.

Of course, "Nameless" would not have written to me if she had not known in her heart what my answer would be. Worse yet, I have the feeling that "Nameless" is painfully aware of having missed her chance.

No Crumbs for the Smart Cookie

Very seldom is the idea of a prenuptial agreement news to the woman who is marrying for the second time.

She may have learned the hard way that such an agreement is as important to her as the marriage license, and without it, she could encounter financial disaster further down the road. Why? For two reasons.

Not only is she just as likely to be employed as is her betrothed, but she could be bringing other assets to their marriage as well. A car, perhaps? Or an apartment, a house, or a savings account. (She may bring even more assets than *he* does.)

But more important, she's already been married once and has learned that—try as hard as you might—you have no assurance that someday you won't be a divorce statistic. That fact alone makes it essential to protect your financial well-being. In fact, many men do. Why not more women?

I have found that most brides over the age of thirty are very tuned-in to such planning for the future. That bride may write to Dear Abby for advice, but usually all that's needed is a word of encouragement:

Dear Abby: I am a thirty-six-year-old divorced woman with two children from a previous marriage. For the last nine years I have been living with a man I love very much. He's forty-six and says he loves me. Last year we purchased a beautiful house in both our names.

My problem is that he has asked me not to work for the last nine years because he wants me "at home." He's an excellent provider, and we lack for nothing. He has told me that I am the beneficiary on all his insurance policies, and I am the main beneficiary in his will.

My concern is his twenty-two-year-old daughter from a previous marriage. What are my legal rights if she contests the will? Could I lose my inheritance fighting the daughter for what is rightfully mine? If he left her a token inheritance, could she still protest?

I love him very much and don't want to leave him, but I need to know that my future will be secure. We've been arguing about this lately because he thinks I'm trying to pressure him into marriage. I would love to be married to him, but could continue to live as we are, as long as I knew his daughter wouldn't take from me what he and I have put together.

Please answer in your column, as I'm sure other women have these questions.

Needs Security

Dear Needs: Please see a lawyer. If your gentleman friend is on the level, he will not object to showing you the documentation (will and insurance policy) you need to feel secure.

Much will depend on how your state recognizes common-law marriage because marriage with a prenuptial agreement may be your best and only protection. You have every right to know.

"Needs Security" is on her way to becoming one smart cookie indeed, and her questions apply for first-time brides, too.

The reason most couples usually avoid such delicate discussions is embarrassment, uneasiness, and in some cases, fear of what they may learn.

Risk it. Both men and women are naive if they don't protect themselves financially.

Frankly, I think any woman or man who brings up the subject shows great personal strength and wisdom—qualities that make for a good marital partner.

These last words on the subject of premarital agreements are not my own. They come from a reader who learned the hard way. Pay attention:

Dear Abby: Some years ago, I married a very wealthy man who asked me to sign a prenuptial agreement. He said he "couldn't" marry me unless I signed it. The agreement not only protected his premarital

27

assets, it prevented me from sharing in any income he earned during our marriage, stipulating what I would receive should we be divorced—and guaranteed me only a pittance in his will.

I hated the agreement, but I loved the man, so I signed it, against the advice of an attorney. I was convinced that I was marrying a fair and generous man, and felt confident that after we were married, he would trash the document.

I was wrong. After many years of marriage, he refused to alter or destroy the agreement, all the while proclaiming his great love for me. He gave me a modest allowance for my personal needs. I bought most of my clothes and even my new car with my earnings. (Yes, I continued to work after my marriage—I was afraid to quit because I felt financially insecure.)

When I finally caught him with another woman (I later learned there had been many), I had the choice of putting up with his philandering, or I could leave empty-handed.

I chose to leave while I was still able to support myself—rather than having him dump me in my old age. I got exactly what the prenuptial agreement stated—except that due to inflation, my pittance of alimony barely pays for my birdseed.

Screwed in San Francisco

"Screwed" says it all.

In *my* wedding book, the prenuptial agreement is a "must" for all brides and grooms, no matter how old they are, whether you are marrying for the first or the fourth time. *But when you draw it up, each party should retain his or her own attorney.* Trust me.

To Spend or Not to Spend

Assuming your relationship survives negotiating that prenuptial agreement, it's still a little too soon to discuss the wedding budget.

First, let's talk about household accounts! We may as well. You'll probably be having this discussion at least once a month for the rest of your married life.

No, no—don't you dare skip ahead to the fun chapters! Stay with me, and look carefully at this preview of what marriage is *really* like.

This is how you can best determine what, how, and when to spend for your wedding.

Chances are you both work. This means that even if your parents are helping with expenses, you are likely to pay a significant portion yourselves.

Or, if you are given a budget by your families to spend on the wedding, as you review your general living costs, you may want to allocate your wedding budget differently. Perhaps spend less on your wedding and put more toward a new car or financing a home. Think it over as you fill in the following:

Basic Monthly Budget

Combined Monthly Income   _____
    Plus
Combined Total Savings   _____

    Total Here   _____

Now subtract:
Rent/Mortgage   _____

Water, Gas, Electricity   _____

Telephone   _____

Car Payments   _____

Loan Payments on Credit Cards   _____

Insurance   _____

Clothing Expenses   _____

Health and Medical Expenses   _____

Transportation   _____

Food and Entertainment   _____

Other   _____

    Total Here   _____

Okay. Now you have a realistic picture of your current financial needs.

Let's look at possible wedding expenses. Many are optional. Keeping your total household budget in mind as you preview wedding expenses may save significant wear and tear on your nerves in the months to come.

Tradition Bound?

Are you an old-fashioned bride and groom? Not likely. But just in case—here's a look at who traditionally pays for what:

The bride's family pays for the ceremony and reception including all invitations, food, liquor, flowers, fees, rentals, photographs, transportation for wedding party, wedding dress and veil, wedding ring and gift for the groom, gifts for the bride's attendants, and hotel accommodations for bridesmaids.

The groom's family pays for the bride's ring, marriage license, bride's bouquet, boutonnieres for the groomsmen, corsages for the mothers and grandmothers, the bride's wedding gift, the honeymoon, and hotel accommodations for the groomsmen.

The rehearsal dinner is usually given by the groom's family but sometimes the bride's family or friends may host it.

Why does the groom pay less? Because in the old days it was assumed that he would take on full financial responsibility for his bride as they drove off, tin cans rattling behind the car, to live happily ever after.

No longer. Today they drive off—still to live happily ever after—but only for a short honeymoon until *both* return to work, to sharing the burden of family finances—both incoming and outgoing.

What makes things different now is the fact that you are a two-career couple. And, even though your families may help, you *both* will share many of the wedding expenses.

Let's look at the big picture in order to plan what works for your personal budget. The magazines say that most weddings cost ten thousand dollars or more, but don't worry if you don't have that kind of money. A lot of people don't.

Remember, this book has been written in order to tell you how to have a beautiful wedding without cashing in all your bonds.

The Wedding Budget

Think about the following and check those expenses you feel you are most likely to have. Don't be afraid to "wish" your first time through the list. There's plenty of time to go back and reconsider each item as you plan.

Record the amount you feel comfortable budgeting in one column. Later, when you have checked costs, record the actual expense, too. Then you can see when you are going over budget.

	Budgeted Cost	Actual Cost
Clothing		
Bride's outfit	_____	_____
Groom's outfit	_____	_____
Ceremony		
Clergy fees	_____	_____
Church rental	_____	_____
Reception		
Caterer/Food	_____	_____
Wedding cake	_____	_____
Bar/Liquor	_____	_____
Site rental	_____	_____
Waiters' tips	_____	_____
Decorations—Centerpieces, Napkins, Etc.	_____	_____
	_____	_____

31

Stationery

    Invitations   _____   _____

    Announcements   _____   _____

    Thank-you notes   _____   _____

Flowers

    Ceremony   _____   _____

    Bride's bouquet   _____   _____

    Bridesmaids' bouquets   _____   _____

    Groom's boutonniere   _____   _____

    Groomsmen's boutonnieres _____   _____

    Mothers' corsages   _____   _____

    Reception arrangements _____   _____

Music

    Wedding   _____   _____

    Reception   _____   _____

    Instrument rentals   _____   _____

    Other   _____   _____

Photography

    Formal portraits   _____   _____

    Candids   _____   _____

32

Videotape   _____   _____

Extra prints   _____   _____

Other   _____   _____

Transportation

Limousines   _____   _____

Travel for out-of-town
  guests   _____   _____

Other   _____   _____

Gifts

Wedding rings   _____   _____

Bride's gift   _____   _____

Groom's gift   _____   _____

Bridal attendants' gifts   _____   _____

Groomsmen's gifts   _____   _____

Other   _____   _____

Rehearsal Dinner

Flowers   _____   _____

Attire   _____   _____

Food   _____   _____

Liquor   _____   _____

Music   _____   _____

Other   _____   _____

Honeymoon

Travel   _____   _____

Accommodations   _____   _____

Wardrobe   _____   _____

Other   _____   _____

Miscellaneous   _____   _____

Marriage license   _____   _____

Bridal consultant   _____   _____

Hotel accommodations for
   out-of-town guests   _____   _____

Other   _____   _____

                                           _____   _____

Wishful Thinking

Now you are facing reality. You are aware of what you would like to do and what you can actually afford to do. You should be felling both relaxed and hopeful. Relaxed, because you are spending only what feels comfortable and makes sense to both of you—and hopeful because you can expect a wonderful life together.

Here's a reader with a new angle on the bridal budget:

Dear Abby: My boyfriend and I want a big church wedding, but we can't afford one, and it would take us four years to save the money, so we have come up with this idea.

We would like to have a Dutch-treat wedding. We could charge $32.60 a couple or $16.30 a person to cover food, drinks, and a portion of the other expenses—like the hall, the music, flowers, table decorations, wedding cake, etc.

I am eighteen and so is my boyfriend. We are both virgins and want to stay that way until we're married.

We wouldn't expect any wedding gifts other than pitching in for the Dutch-treat wedding.

I don't know how much longer we can wait, Abby.

Don't you think a lot of folks would pay $32.60 a couple toward getting two good Christians married?

Thank you for any advice you can give us.

In Love in West Virginia

Dear In Love: You'll never know until you ask. Poll your friends and you'll have your answer.

Naturally, I had dozens of letters from folks either agreeing or heartily appalled by my response. I stand by my response—do what works for you and your friends.

On the other hand, don't go too far:

Dear Abby: I sure need advice in a hurry regarding wedding reception protocol. I am being married in two weeks. My fiancé and I are paying for everything ourselves. Not easily by a long shot, but it's by our choice.

The problem is that in the latter part of the wedding reception, we thought we would pass "the hat" for any donations people wish to give to help us start our married life a little easier after such a big expense.

My mother and sister are appalled at this suggestion! They say it is very tacky and of low class, and you just don't do it this way. They say that if we couldn't afford a wedding, we shouldn't have one.

I have been to very few weddings, but some did pass the hat and some did not. I found it neither improper nor tacky.

Please answer in the paper because, like myself, my mom reads your column regularly and this is not a topic I wish to discuss with her again (unless necessary) to save an argument. Thank you.

Not Wanting to Be Tacky

Dear Not: Passing the hat in my opinion would be tacky. Pass the idea—forget the hat.

I have always believed that the purpose of a wedding was to exchange vows before friends and relatives with whom the couple wanted to share their joy.

Conjugal Commonsense

Two basic rules should guide your decisions: First, make this a wedding tailored exclusively for you. Don't try to imitate what your best friend did. Don't feel that you must have a big wedding to make your mother, your mother-in-law, or anyone except yourselves happy. You two are making the memories. Do it your way.

Second, consider what's most important to you. A bridal consultant who helped her three daughters stage lovely weddings, each one different from the other, offers these words of wisdom as both a professional wedding planner and the mother of the bride.

> Determine what you most want for that special day. One of my daughters felt her priority was inviting lots of people, so we planned an event that allowed us to keep our costs lower for the location, the food, and the extras.
>
> I saved money by putting myself in charge of the food and liquor.
>
> Another daughter had always wanted to be married at a very swanky place, so we budgeted for that first, then cut costs in other areas. She invited fewer people, we had a trio instead of a full band, and served drinks and finger foods instead of a sit-down dinner.
>
> But whatever we did—the moment you entered the church or the reception—you could tell instantly which of my daughters was being married. Each one has a distinct personality which was clearly evident on her wedding day!

Incidentally, the mother pointed out that the services of a bridal consultant are needed not only for expensive weddings. Her duties might range from helping a bride plan every detail up to the final event, to just being at the church on the wedding day to insure no one steps on her train.

A bridal consultant's fee, therefore, can be very reasonable and depend entirely on what a bride and groom might require.

Sometimes the bridal budget prompts a different concern:

Dear Abby: I'll get right to the point. If a couple has lived together for about a year, are they entitled to a big wedding?

Needs to Know

Dear Needs: They are entitled to any kind of wedding they can afford.

Need I say more?

Love Is Wonderful the Second Time Around

More questions are being asked about second marriages than ever before. Here's one that shows up almost daily in my mail:

Dear Abby: Our daughter is going to be married for the second time. We paid for her first wedding. Her husband died five years ago. Who pays for her second wedding?

Mom and Pop

Dear Mom and Pop: Your daughter and her fiancé. Parents are not expected to pay for a second wedding. Some don't even pay for the first.

That answer holds for *almost* every second marriage. I learned a long time ago never to say "*this* is exactly how things should be," as someone invariably throws me a curve.

Dear Abby: Our son, forty-two, is getting married for the second time. His first marriage ended in divorce nine years ago. The woman he's marrying is twenty-two, and this is her first marriage.

Her parents are planning a large church wedding with all the trimmings—the kind our son had the first time. What part do we play in this wedding?

It's seventeen years later and our lifestyle has changed considerably. My husband is retired, and we are in much more modest circumstances now. We hosted one lavish rehearsal dinner the night before the wedding, as is customary for the groom's parents, but we are in no position to do it again. The bride's parents are fine people—younger

37

and better off financially than we are.

We want a good rapport with them, so please tell us how to handle this.

Parents of the Groom

Dear Parents: Explain your circumstances candidly to the bride's parents. Don't do any more than you can comfortably afford. Parents who have participated in one wedding have paid their dues, and are exempt from the obligations of repeat performances.

Elopement: A Comfortable Classic

You need not do the conventional, you know. Some folks love the peace and quiet and low cost of the classic elopement. You can always follow the announcement of your marriage with a small reception in your home or apartment for just a few close friends or your family.

Some folks do not want a lot of fanfare. They're more comfortable doing things with as little hoopla as possible.

And, for those of you interested in the old stepladder to the window routine—I've had the wedding abroad brought to my attention recently.

"Our families both lived so far away that wherever we chose to be married, it was going to be hard on someone," said a groom of my acquaintance. His bride, who could get only a week off from work, had always dreamed of honeymooning in Paris.

"We were married in a civil ceremony in our hometown," said the bride, "so we wouldn't have to hassle with residency requirements, then we had the loveliest service in a little chapel in the country outside Paris. It was so romantic."

The parents of both the bride and groom gave them money as wedding gifts, which paid for their honeymoon. Then, when they returned, the couple hosted a small party for friends and family and showed slides of their trip!

"It was a dream come true," said the bride. "We had a fascinating week together and it was a gift! Our wedding ceremony couldn't have been more memorable."

The Preacher's Lament

If my mail is an accurate "behavior barometer," many couples overlook one crucial item as they make out their budget: the fee for the clergy.

I receive dozens of letters a year from these folks who seem to be taken for granted by wedding couples:

Dear Abby: I am a minister. A few days ago, I performed a wedding for a couple who attend my congregation. I worked with this couple for three months prior to the wedding, in preparation for the event. This included premarital counseling, helping them write their vows, arranging the rehearsal, and finally, performing the ceremony. The wedding came off beautifully.

So what's the problem? I didn't get paid a cent! The photographer was paid. The man who took the video was paid. The florist was paid, and so was the organist and the caterers.

I can't understand why the minister is supposed to perform the service for free. Should I have sent them a bill?

I would like to know how other ministers handle this.

Left Standing at the Altar

That was the first letter. After I ran it in my column, this one arrived with a different point of view:

Dear Abby: This concerns the minister who felt left out because he was not paid for having officiated at a wedding, as were the photographer, florist, organist, and caterer. He could not understand why he was expected to perform the marriage service for free. He asked advice from other ministers.

I have been an Episcopal (Anglican) priest for twenty-eight years, and have never charged for solemnizing a wedding (or any other ministration). Indeed, I have always told couples that I had no fee, expected none, and wanted none.

My reason? Officiating at weddings, baptisms, funerals, etc., is what my parish pays me to do. Requesting or accepting fees in addition to my salary (not large, but adequate) is, I believe, morally wrong, as my ministrations are part of God's free gift to us all.

When a person insisted on giving me a money gift for my services, I put the money into my discretionary fund to help the poor and others in need. Yours faithfully,

The Reverend John L. Wolff

But his was not the last word:

Dear Abby: Listen to this! When my husband and I went for our first meeting with our minister, at the close of our appointment, we were handed an envelope. Inside was a "statement" that read:

1. Minister and use of church	$350
2. Clean-up following ceremony	$25
3. Organist	$35
4. Soloist	$25

To be paid one week prior to wedding.

This may be hard for some people to swallow, but at least they know what everything is going to cost.

Liz and Bill

It is as I always suspected: There is no free wedding.

Love, Abby

3

Avoid a Nuptial Nightmare: Plan Ahead

Planning is essential. No bridal couple wants to spend their wedding day worrying about details. Those precious moments when you exchange your vows should be exactly that—a time to think of just you two.

Anxiety over cakes and caterers, gowns and guests, belongs to another day. So let's talk about planning.

Rules for the Ruthless Wedding Planner

And while some may call you ruthless, I will call you wise if you remember to organize, organize, organize.

Planning every single detail of your wedding is the only way you can successfully pull off an event that involves as many people, places, and emotions as a wedding.

Rule Number One—Know what is right for you.

Begin with your image of the perfect wedding, but be realistic about time, location, and finances.

Keep your arrangements easy to manage. If a family affair is important to you, have you chosen a site fairly close to family members? If it's the rainy season, are you gambling on an outdoor event? Be wary of holidays when parades or community events could hamper your plans.

Most important, think over how much time the bride, the groom, and others who may be involved will have to spend on planning and execution.

Rule Number Two—Keep detailed lists.

You will find a "Wedding Countdown" in the back of this book. Here I have listed—by category—a checklist of everything you may be planning to include in your wedding.

This "Wedding Countdown" has been set up for a three-month schedule, which you can adapt if you have slightly more, or slightly less, time. The categories include the following:

1. Budget
2. Ceremony
3. Bride and groom wardrobes
4. Transportation
5. Flowers
6. Music
7. Photos
8. Reception
9. Stationery
10. Guests
11. Gifts
12. Wedding party
13. Honeymoon
14. Miscellaneous

In addition, there are *two* cut-out lists—one for the bride and one for the groom—for each of you to keep with you over the coming weeks.

As you plan your "Wedding Countdown," you should mark each item with the initials of the person responsible and add that to your individual lists. Now you have your own schedules, plus a master list to keep everyone and everything coordinated.

Rule Number Three—Check your lists regularly.

Take time each week to go over the master list and update each other on what has been accomplished, what is running late and what remains to be done. As you get closer to the date, you will want to do this daily.

This is the time to keep each other informed of budget matters and other changes you may need to make.

Rule Number Four—Get help.

You can't do everything yourselves. Do you need a bridal consultant to take charge of a few things—or everything—for you? If so, talk with two or three, and choose the one you find most compatible.

When faced with a dilemma over a decision, consult an expert.

Do you have a family member willing to help out? Many mothers of brides—and grooms—are happy to be a part of the plans. However, that leads me directly to:

Rule Number Five—No bride, no groom, no parent should be involved with any of the details on the day of the wedding. That's mandatory!

You can be involved in every tiny decision up to, but excluding, the wedding day. And that goes *especially* for the mothers of the bride and the groom.

I suggest you find a close friend whom you can "brief" shortly before the wedding. Ask this person to be the "manager of the day" so that bride, groom, and all parents are free to enjoy the celebration. Nor should the person be either the best man or maid of honor. Select someone not in the wedding party.

This is important! If anyone needs to be free of worry on the day of the wedding, it's the bride, the groom, and their families.

Sound easy? It is—thanks to good planning.

The One-Minute Marriage

Of course, no one can get married "in a minute," but there will always be a few who will try to put a wedding together in one week.

If that's you, then here are a few suggestions:

Day One—Surprise everyone with your announcement. Telephone— or tell a talkative friend. Suggest that your parents and friends handle their hysteria with smelling salts or deep breathing. After they have recovered, ask the party of your choice if you can have a small ceremony and reception at their place unless you have a place of your own that can handle ten or twelve people.

43

Day Two—Get that blood test.
        Select a wedding dress and maid of honor.
        (Note: The best man is selected by the groom.)
        Invite close family and friends.
        Find a judge, clergyperson, or justice of the peace.
        You may have to consider city hall, too. Check the times and legal requirements.

Day Three—Complete applications for the wedding license.
        Plan and buy food, champagne, and flowers.

Days Four and Five—Make sure you have the legal ends covered.
        Arrange for *serving* of food and champagne.
        Pick up flowers.

Day Six—Enjoy "rehearsal" dinner with friends and family.
        Retire early in preparation for the big day.

Day Seven—Rejoice! You really did it.

Love, Abby

4

Brave New Weddings

The time has come to set the stage! What kind of ceremony will you have?

Will yours be a traditional wedding? Or one that is likely to knock the socks off the old folks? Will it be at the altar of a venerable, historic church? Or set in the soft morning mists of a hidden valley? Will you be wed at home or abroad?

Whatever your choice, you can do it! That's what's so wonderful about today's "brave new weddings"—*anything goes!* Do it your way.

A Ceremony "Sampler"

Should you worry that your plans might be too "nontraditional," I encourage you to read this lovely essay that was recently brought to my attention. It was written by Carolyn R. Flint of the *Hartford Courant*. Her words tell all:

> When I was a bride-to-be, almost thirty years ago, I told my mother that my fiancé and I wanted to be married in a Quaker meeting house in a neighboring town. My mother demurred, saying, "Pastor would be offended."
>
> From that moment on, I may have been the main character, but I was

not in charge of my wedding. While I look back on that day as one of great happiness, it was not one of great meaning to me.

Last summer I attended five wonderful weddings: daughters of friends, relatives, and neighbors. I felt the bride's influence in all of the ceremonies, and most of the services had parts written by both the bride and groom. The array of choices for music, vows, and people involved was amazing. Feminists have always stressed that women should have options, and, believe me, there are options for weddings today.

One wedding had a traditional look to it: bride in white, proud father and mother, Episcopal service, bridesmaids, ushers, and young ring-bearer. But we all knew that the ring-bearer was the son of the groom. This new family was starting out together at the church altar. The ring-bearer, who is deaf, signed a message to his father at one point, and was given a quick sign in reply from his father, and a slightly longer one from his new mother. I felt proud to witness the commitment this couple was making, not only to each other, but to their son.

A second wedding had an untraditional processional. First, the parents of the bride and groom came down the two side aisles, then the bridesmaids came down one side while the ushers came down the other. Finally, the bride walked down one aisle and the groom came down another one, all to the music of a harpsichord and flute. Yet the prayers were traditional; the bride will submit to her husband, and the husband will submit to Christ. These words, however, were written by the bride and groom as an expression of their faith.

A third wedding was impressive in its outreach. A traditional Catholic service with a beautiful bride in a white veil and long train emphasized joy and thanks. Thanksgiving was demonstrated by a basket of food gifts that would be given to the needy. A Lutheran minister was also asked to bless the couple, and he, in turn, thanked the priest for this privilege. The love of this couple seemed to ripple outwards to include those of us in the congregation and others outside the church.

The fourth wedding was for the immediate family only, but the reception the next day was for friends and guests. This couple persuaded motel owners to hold the wedding and reception under a tent by the shores of Lake Champlain. The bride's father, who is a justice of the peace in another state, performed the wedding ceremony, and it was legalized by a local justice of the peace. The bride's dress had been made by a friend, and each hand-lettered wedding invitation included a piece of the lace used for the dress. (In return, the bride had made the wedding cake for the seamstress's reception.) The spirit of care and cooperation highlighted this wedding.

The final wedding of the season appeared completely traditional: the white Congregational church in the center of a small New England town, the usual procession, church vows repeated after the minister, hymns and prayers listed in a program. But on the back of the program was a definition of love as found in a "Calvin and Hobbes" comic strip—a dash of humor that brought a smile to the face of many middle-aged friends. Maybe that bit of jollity contributed to people of all ages dancing heartily to rock music during the reception.

These brides seemed to have clear ideas about who they are. They were allowed to express their own ideas about love, marriage, and relationships in their ceremonies. Having options within the services let them show their distinct personalities.

I suspect these brides will not only remember the happiness of their wedding days, but they will recall the ways the ceremonies reflected their own thinking at that time. What a much more meaningful way to start a lifetime of commitment.

I want to repeat what Carolyn said so well—those wonderful weddings mirrored perfectly the feelings and beliefs and everyday lives of the couples involved. But they did something else, too. They were easily attended and understood—even participated in—by the guests. That should be your goal.

Many couples who set out to plan a wedding experience some confusion over the ceremony and, in particular, the social role of the clergy likely to be involved.

After many letters and responses appearing in my column—here's a letter that clarifies one of the more subtle issues that bothers many couples during the initial stages of planning:

Dear Abby: As a member of the clergy, I am asking you to print this on behalf of those of us who are asked to officiate at weddings.

I have been told that it is customary for pastors to attend both the rehearsal dinner and the reception. Others have told me that they invite the pastor only because they think they have to. I've been told by some folks that they would prefer that the pastor didn't attend the rehearsal dinner.

I am aware of the expense involved in having a wedding. I'm also aware that some folks feel awkward around clergy, so I am calling

47

upon you, Dear Abby, to tell couples to be straightforward about their expectations.

I enjoy wedding festivities, but I would like to know in advance whether I'm invited. I am not married, and I often end up attending alone when I would have enjoyed bringing a friend.

My married clergy friends say they never know whether their wives or husbands are invited to the rehearsal dinner and wedding reception.

So, Abby, the questions many clergy would like to have answered are:

1. Do you want me to be present at the rehearsal dinner?
2. Do you want me to be present at your wedding reception?
3. May I bring my spouse or a friend?

Abby, I cannot count the number of times I am half out the door following a wedding rehearsal when the bride runs after me saying, "Aren't you staying for the dinner?" (I wasn't invited.)

Any advice you can give us would be appreciated.

Confused Clergyperson

Let's clear up the confusion here and now.

To those of you who are planning a wedding: When you ask a clergyperson to officiate, your request does not automatically include invitations to the wedding festivities. If you want to include the clergyperson—and spouse or friend—extend an invitation.

Many couples have told me that they want their clergyperson to attend the festivities, but they're afraid if they send a formal invitation the recipients will feel obligated to send a gift, which would be a financial burden considering the number of weddings they attend.

I advise them to extend the invitation *by telephone*. It's not as formal as sending an engraved invitation in the mail, which more or less suggests a gift is expected.

Now that you know how to include the clergy in your plans—it's time to discover how they work you into *theirs*.

Don't Hesitate—Investigate!

Dear Abby: I'm Jewish and she's Japanese—what kind of ceremony should we have?

Bewildered

Dear Bewildered: You can change your religion, but she will always be Japanese. Unless one of you is willing to compromise, I recommend a civil ceremony.

Some sleuthing may be necessary before you decide on your clergy and/or ceremony because some clergy in different religions have specific requirements. Some require counseling, instruction or conversion before the wedding ceremony.

You will be wise to check on this immediately upon selecting your wedding date as some clergy may require several months of preparation prior to the wedding.

A more frequent dilemma is that facing couples of different religions:

Dear Abby: Please print this for people who want to marry outside their religion, because that is our situation and we don't know which way to turn.

We are both twenty-one and in college. I was raised a Roman Catholic and the girl I want to marry was raised a Jew. We love each other and never once have argued over religion. However, her parents aren't too happy about her marrying a Catholic, and my parents aren't exactly thrilled with my marrying a Jew.

I have no desire to turn Jewish, and my fiancée doesn't want to turn Catholic. We want to be married in either a church or a synagogue, but no priest will marry us, and neither will a rabbi. Who will, then?

If we have children, we plan to expose them to both religions and let them decide what they want to be. Any ideas?

In Love in Boston

Dear In Love: If there's a rabbi or a Roman Catholic priest who will perform a mixed marriage in a synagogue or church, I don't know where he (or she) is.

You may have to settle for a civil ceremony, but if you want a religious ceremony, try one of the Unitarian Universalist churches in your area.

Well, did my advice to "In Love" precipitate a response! Three more letters arrived hot on the heels of that column and all three are packed with valuable information. Read on!

Dear Abby: In a recent column you stated: "If there is a rabbi or Roman Catholic priest who will perform a mixed marriage in a synagogue or church, I don't know where he (or she) is." Permit me to reply.

There are many rabbis and many priests who will officiate. We have had many mixed marriages in our synagogue in the past several years, including many in which clergy of other faiths have participated in the wedding ceremony.

Furthermore, the Rabbinic Center of Research and Counseling in Westfield, New Jersey, periodically compiles a list of rabbis who will officiate at interfaith marriages. There are presently 180 rabbis on that list, including more than fifty who will invite other clergy to join them in the ceremony.

Rabbi John M. Sherwood,
Temple Emet,
Woodland Hills, California

Rabbi Sherwood's advice was most appreciated. However, do not assume you can ring up any rabbi on the list mentioned and be assured of an instant marriage ceremony.

For example, most rabbis require a premarital conference and encourage a program of Jewish study after the marriage. Some rabbis (not all) require a commitment that the couple will establish a Jewish home and/or raise their children in the Jewish faith.

There are other conditions too numerous to mention here, but a national list of rabbis who will perform mixed marriages, plus the prerequisites of each, is available free of charge by writing to:

> Rabbi Irwin H. Fishbein
> Rabbinic Center for Research and Counseling
> 128 East Dudley Avenue
> Westfield, New Jersey 07090

That's letter Number One. Here's Number Two:

Dear Abby: Thank you for recommending the Unitarian Church to the Catholic man and Jewish woman who wanted to marry but couldn't find a priest or rabbi who would perform the ceremony.

My Catholic daughter was engaged to a Jewish man, and they, too, were having trouble finding a clergyman of either faith to marry them. They were ready to settle for a justice of the peace when in your column I read about a couple who was having the same problem. You said, "Try the Unitarian Church."

I called my daughter immediately and she got right on it. She found a Unitarian Church listed in the phone book, called and made an appointment with the minister. Then she and her fiancé went to see him.

First, he gave them a course in premarital counseling, and then he married them in a beautiful ceremony that included both the Christian and the Jewish rituals.

I hope the couple who wrote to you takes your advice and finds a Unitarian minister as wonderful as theirs. I have never attended a more beautiful wedding nor heard a more meaningful service.

Mrs. D. Craig,
Magnolia, New Jersey

And, last but not least, here's advice that can be followed no matter *who* you are or *where* you live:

Dear Abby: Those in the New York area should investigate the Chapel of the United Nations. It's a beautiful setting!

Elsewhere, inquire at the nearest college or university. A rabbi and a priest can be found to perform the ceremony at a nondenominational chapel where the dignity and spirituality of both religions are combined. You don't have to be a young college kid to be married in a chapel on a college campus. Anyone of legal age—and up—can get married there.

Hitched at the Hillel House

There, lots of alternatives to take care of the religious side of the blessed event.

How About Other Options?

The only limit is your imagination. Even the altar site can offer an opportunity for something quite different. I recently attended a wedding ceremony in which a large mirror had been set up so that the faces of the bride and groom were visible to the guests during the ceremony. It was lovely and very moving to see their expressions as they pledged their love to one another.

Some folks "go further." I received a letter from a couple who wanted to be married in flight by an airline captain!

Dear Abby: My husband and I were married on March 4, 1974, by the Reverend Wayne Bryan, a Baptist minister from Baton Rouge, on a Delta Airlines flight between Baton Rouge and Shreveport, Louisiana. We reserved the first-class section and brought along the entire wedding party.

It was a second marriage for both of us. We had been married (to each other) a year before, in Charleston, West Virginia, but because of a legal technicality we needed a Louisiana marriage license.

The captain announced the marriage to the rest of the passengers, and Delta furnished the champagne and flowers.

Dr. and Mrs. Jean Jeffus,
New Orleans

Is It Different the Second Time Around?

The previous letter introduces a common dilemma: What *is* appropriate for the second marriage. The following letter is typical of many I receive:

Dear Abby: "Linda" and I are planning to marry. This will be my first and Linda's second. (I am thirty and she is twenty-seven.) When Linda was twenty-one, she was married for sixteen months, then her marriage was annulled. I have accepted this and have never made an issue of it.

I think we should have a simple church ceremony, but Linda wants a repeat of her first wedding—bridesmaids, bridal gown, escorted down the aisle on her father's arm to "Here Comes the Bride"—virtually ignoring the fact that she was once married. She insists that the dissolution "erased" her former marriage and she's entitled to a traditional church wedding. All the etiquette books I have read support my opinion.

Your opinion, please.

Uneasy in Ohio

Dear Uneasy: An annulment does not "erase" a marriage. But more important than what the etiquette books say is the fact that Linda refuses to consider your wishes in the matter.

Today, many brides who marry for a second time (or third) do have traditional church weddings, but only if their first was an understated, simple one. Linda should consult with the clergyperson who will perform the ceremony. I think he or she will vote with you.

The bottom line? Your second (or third or fourth) marriage is for family and close friends *only*.

What If You Have Been Living Together?

After much debate in my column, I offer the final word on this question from one who knows:

> Dear Abby: I am writing about the couple signed "Making It Legal." They have lived together for eleven years, have two children, ages ten and three, and a third due in September. Now they want to make it legal with a formal church wedding in December, which they can pay for themselves.
>
> Family members stated that after eleven years and three children, that kind of wedding would be inappropriate, so the couple asked for your opinion. You disappointed me when you sided with the family. Abby, being a minister and having performed many weddings, may I offer my input?
>
> I see no reason why this couple shouldn't have the kind of wedding they want. It would make them happy, and would be hurting no one. They would be most welcome in my church, and their children could even be part of the service.
>
> Last Saturday, I officiated at a formal church wedding. The bride was eight months pregnant. We threw puffed rice!
>
> The Reverend John St. Dennis,
Hi-Desert Church of Religious Science,
Apple Valley, California

> Dear John St. Dennis: You win. My mail has been overwhelmingly in favor of letting the couple have the kind of wedding they want. Score: "Making It Legal," 467; Abby, 19.

Critical Details

In the midst of all these plans, brides and grooms frequently forget that certain legal details must be attended to. Check with your clergyperson or the official who will perform the service.

Legal Legwork:
1. Arrange for the blood test.

2. Apply for your marriage license at the clerk's office of the town in which you will be wed. A fee is charged, and there may be a waiting period.
3. Check for other legal regulations in the location of your ceremony. If you choose to be married abroad, it may be more complicated.
4. Will either of you be changing your name? Be sure to make changes with the Social Security Administration and any other property or legal documents.
5. Have you been previously married? If so, you will need your divorce documents for proof of divorce.

Health Tips

Prior to your wedding, more medical information than just a blood test may be required—especially for the bride. Be sure to see your doctor (preferably a gynecologist) for a physical check-up and authoritative answers to all your questions well before your marriage.

If birth control is desired, it should be planned—and discussed by the bride and groom—before the wedding. Too many young wives, who have planned on working for a few years, discover to their great surprise that they got pregnant on their honeymoon. (Yes, many girls assume that they cannot get pregnant the "first" time.)

Also, many couples have experienced shock and grief on learning that they were unable to consummate their marriage due to some slight physical abnormality that might have been easily corrected with minor surgery before the wedding.

Please note, readers, that motherly advice from "Aunt Liz" or "tips" from one of the girls from work are fine, but before a bride keeps her date with the preacher, she should keep at least one more date—with her doctor.

♥

Dear Abby's Steps to a Successful Ceremony

1. Decide on the type and style of your wedding ceremony.
   This is the time to think about how you might personalize your

ceremony. Consider each of the following and research those that you may want to do "your own way": The procession, prayers, groom's vows, bride's vows, giving-away of the bride, bride's and groom's exchange of the rings, special readings, music, candle-lighting, the kiss, or closing of the ceremony, recessional, the inclusion of family members or friends in the ceremony. Jot down your ideas here:

_____

_____

_____

_____

_____

_____

_____

_____

_____

_____

_____

_____

_____

_____

2. Contact the appropriate clergy to set date. List names, addresses, phone numbers:

_____

_____

_____

_____

_____

_____

_____

_____

3. Request all necessary information regarding costs (location *and* clergy). List here or with budget:

_____

_____

_____

_____

_____

_____

_____

4. Check to see if religious preparation is needed and schedule accordingly. List dates:

_____

_____

_____

_____

_____

5. Decide whether to invite clergy to other festivities and inform clergy of your expectations. Add names to guest list.

_____

_____

_____

_____

_____

6. Make list of other accoutrements needed for the ceremony such as music and flowers. Do you need to arrange for these, or will the clergy/church/synagogue handle these arrangements? List here:

_____

_____

_____

_____

_____

7. Check legal requirements of your ceremony/location. List here:

_____

_____

_____

_____

_____

8. Double-check public events that might be scheduled at that time and near the location of your ceremony for possible conflicts in scheduling that could cause problems. List here:

_____

_____

_____

_____

_____

9. List any unusual plans you have that will require special follow-through. List here:

_____

_____

_____

_____

_____

_____

10. Arrange for blood tests, marriage license applications, medical check-ups, legal advice. List dates, time, place, and records needed (birth certificates, divorce documents, passports, etc.):

_____

_____

_____

_____

_____

_____

_____

_____

_____

5

Shall We Dance?
Time to Select
Your Music and Flowers,
Cameras and Cars,
Caterer and Cake

It's time to plan the fun stuff! Time to select, budget, and schedule all the details that add up to a delightful, never-to-be-forgotten wedding ceremony and reception.

Begin by sitting down together to review once more *where* you want to spend your money. How much you have budgeted for: The wedding? The honeymoon? Your future home?

Sure of everything? Probably not.

If you are like any one of the thousands of brides and grooms who have written to me over the last thirty years for advice on items as minor as your "something borrowed," or as major as the proper way to seat your divorced parents, you are likely to have dozens of questions.

Most people learn from their own mistakes. The smart ones learn from the mistakes of others. For example:

Chris Thomas of Dallas was wed recently. She and her husband, Robert, celebrated with a wedding their families will always remember (for more reasons than you may think!), and she shared their experience in this piece she wrote for the *Dallas Morning News:*

> Once my fiancé, Robert, and I decided to take the marital plunge, we pored over the endless list of wedding details that makes *every sane couple* think twice about going through the whole thing.

But at ages thirty-two and twenty-eight, it seemed ludicrous to have our parents arrange and pay for everything. We wanted it to be our big day in every respect.

We had been to plenty of lovely catered wedding fetes, but they didn't really fit the classy but casual style we had envisioned. When we decided to spend most of our cash on a European honeymoon instead of hors d'oeuvres and cake, we knew we needed "elegance on a budget." We hoped that if we catered our own reception, we'd get what we wanted, with money to spare.

So we sat down one afternoon and started making notes:

How many people would be invited? (About eighty.)

What time of day? (2 to 5 P.M.)

What utensils and appliances would be needed?

We listed every item we could think of, from tables to trash bags, then broke it down into three more lists:

> What to rent
> What to buy or borrow
> Whom to hire

We decided right away to have the wedding cake made. For the rest of the food, we called on about a dozen good friends who had said, "If there's anything I can do to help, let me know."

Several had complained that they didn't know what to give us as wedding gifts. "What we really need is your time and your best recipes," I told them. (Lest mothers and mothers-in-law feel left out, remind them that they are at the top of the Helpers' List.)

When you have chosen your helpers, invite them for brunch and a big planning session. We termed our menu "heavy hors d'oeuvres," since we planned to supply enough finger foods to satisfy even the hungriest guest.

The helpers were full of ideas: One makes world-class stuffed mushrooms; another's specialty is an unusual egg-and-shrimp dip. We sought dishes that could be made in advance, with a variety of flavors and colors. A friend who wailed that she wasn't good at anything was assigned the duty of finding (and washing) the most beautiful strawberries, and providing confectioners' sugar to dip them in.

We estimated each guest would eat ten hors d'oeuvres, so we had eight hundred pieces to make. (Incidentally, we wound up with too much food.) Dividing that by the number of helpers, we assigned each five dozen pieces. When the mothers came to town, they too donned aprons and met their quotas, which gave them less time to fuss over the bride and groom.

On the day of the wedding, the instructions were specific: Deliver your dish in a disposable container between 11 A.M. and noon to the reception site. Have a capable, well-organized friend—not a member of the wedding party—act as coordinator, armed with a master checklist of food items and serving instructions.

Another friend carried envelopes containing checks to pay the wait staff and musicians. My dad had a copy of the rental contract for the tables, linen, silver, and glassware. His instructions were to meet the rental company at the party room the next day, when they picked everything up.

What about libations? We decided a wet bar was too complicated and potentially pricey. Robert and his friends took responsibility for selecting, buying, and chilling wine, champagne, and soft drinks; coffee was made and served in a silver urn.

We could hardly transform the party room of our new townhouse into Wedding Wonderland, but a balloon company provided a perfect alternative to a big florist's bill. The balloon man virtually covered the place with pink-and-green balloons and streamers. A dozen pink roses stood on each serving table. We were surprised how far our decorating budget stretched.

Did everything go as planned? Well—not exactly. We forgot entirely about buying a special knife to cut the cake and had to make do with the big kitchen variety. The cake was fully twice the size we needed—not everyone eats it—and the picture-perfect rolled fondant icing was at least half an inch thick and thoroughly unappetizing.

Those were minor problems, but every wedding has a Big Disaster. Ours came after the reception, when Robert and I were winging our way to London. Looking back on that day, it was a simple case of misunderstanding.

The staff we hired to "set out, serve, and clean up" didn't perform the last task quite the way we expected. To us, "clean up" meant they would leave the room exactly as we rented it—vacuumed, dusted, spotlessly clean. But they were servers, not janitors; we should not have expected them to do double-duty. They rinsed dishes, stacked everything nicely . . . and left.

Our poor parents ended up hauling trash bags and scouring restrooms long after the guests had departed.

That's how it went. Once in a while, Robert and I bring out the wedding album and relive that special day. We think our close friends especially enjoyed our reception because they were truly part of its success. Our only regret—besides saddling our parents with last-minute janitorial duties—is that we had to leave the best party we ever gave in order to make the plane!

Despite the snafu, Chris and Robert had a terrific celebration. Even the "big disaster" has become one of their fondest memories.

So plan your celebration *your* way. Let's begin.

"Get Me to the Church (and Reception) on Time!"

Transportation is essential. Whether you want a Rolls-Royce limousine, a horse-powered buggy, a "stretch" Lincoln Town Car, or trusty Toyotas borrowed from friends—make your reservations early.

♥

Transportation Checklist

1. How many and what kind of cars do you need? For example, how many cars for your parents, the groom's parents, your attendants, and yourselves. List here:

_____

_____

_____

_____

(Please check this again one month before your wedding as this number is likely to change. You may plan only for attendants now and learn later that you need cars for other relatives and friends. Establish deadlines for final count.)

2. Get at least two estimates from different rental services. If you are looking for the unusual, try your local vintage car clubs, someone may have a classic car for the bride and groom. Does the rental cost include a tip or is a tip also expected? List rental services or drivers here. Include names and phone numbers.

_____

_____

_____

_____

_____

3. Plan for:
a. The schedule. Prepare a checklist for each driver that lists the people to be picked up and their addresses with necessary directions; the different locations and directions; the times of arrival. Double-check to be sure each driver has the correct list. Record a master schedule here:

_____

_____

_____

_____

_____

_____

_____

_____

b. Refreshments on board, i.e., champagne from the church to reception? If so, do you need insurance in the event such refreshments are spilled or the rental cars are damaged in any way?

c. If you are asking friends to drive you in their cars, offer to pay for gas and a car wash. (They'll probably refuse, but offer anyway.)

d. Add other details here.

_____

_____

_____

_____

"Picture Perfect"

Flowers—This is one item that can really run up the bill on your wedding.

One bride of my acquaintance told her caterer that she could spend only half of what he had suggested as a budget—and what do you think cut the cost in half? Changing the flower arrangements! More is not necessarily better. Witness the prize-winning Japanese floral arrangements—fewer flowers, gracefully arranged.

As you plan your ceremony, check to see what flowers, if any, are allowed. Often, only the altar and aisle posts are decorated. On the other hand, for the reception, you can usually do as much as your budget allows, but book that florist *immediately* upon setting your wedding date!

If you're on a very tight budget, you may want to consider doing the flowers yourself (with the help of an artistic friend who will undertake the physical work and set it all up on your wedding day). Or how about this lucky bride?

> Dear Abby: I was recently married for the second time and something wonderful happened that might charm some of your readers into doing the same.
>
> One of my closest friends, who knew that my fiancé and I were on a very tight budget because we both have children from our first marriages, asked if her gift to us could be the flowers for our wedding,

including my bridal bouquet!

I still get misty-eyed when I recall what she did: Since we were wed May 1 in our own backyard, my "flower friend" sent a florist in to plant budding tulips in the grass where our ceremony was to take place. Other pots of spring blooms were set throughout the house and on the patio.

My bouquet was a lovely cascade of tulips and irises and the groom was given a small pink rose to wear on his lapel. At the home of yet another friend, where we had our reception, a bouquet cascaded from a wicker basket hung on the front door.

Those flowers were a gift I remember with great affection every time I open my wedding album.

Enchanted in Kansas

Dear Kansas: What an elegant gift! And one you are sure to cherish always, though the blooms may have been fleeting.

Another thought for the bride who is marrying for the second time: If your celebration will be a quiet family affair, why not consider silk flowers? A stunning arrangement in a silver bowl for the ceremony— and one or two long-stemmed beauties to be carried by you—will add a stylish note to your wedding and become a lasting memento as part of your home decor.

♥ ♥ DEAR ABBY RED ALERT ♥ ♥

The time to talk flowers is also the time to talk *rice.* A traditional "decoration" of the bridal pair, rice has fallen into disuse because it leaves marks on wooden floors, is difficult to clean up from sidewalks, easy to slip on, and is considered by some to be a poor diet for birds.

My suggestion? Birdseed. It feels the same on the bridal brow, ruffles few feathers among the clergy who are protective of their premises, and is a treat for the local fowl.

Nor does it have to come out of plastic bags. Using the extra fabric from her bridesmaids' gowns, one bride made tiny rosebuds into which she tucked the birdseed. Then "roses" were handed out as her wedding reception came to a close.

67

♥

Wedding Flower Checklist

1. Set budget—Do you need flowers for both ceremony and reception? List your requirements here:

_____

_____

2. Select florist—Record name and phone number; record dates for final confirmation.

_____

_____

3. Meet with florist to decide on arrangement styles—traditional or contemporary—for the following:
   a. Church decorations

_____

_____

   b. Reception arrangements (Keep centerpieces low so guests can see one another across table.)

_____

_____

   c. Bridal bouquet and bouquets for bridesmaids (Take fabric swatch to conference with florist if you wish to match flowers to your gowns.)
   Bride:

_____

_____

Bridesmaids:

_____

_____

Flowergirl:

_____

_____

d. Boutonnieres for groom and groomsmen

_____

_____

e. Corsages, etc., for mothers of bride and groom and other relatives

_____

_____

f. Aisle runner for procession into church—most florists provide this on request

_____

_____

g. Decide what to do with flowers after the ceremony. Hospitals? Nursing homes?

_____

_____

h. Rice vs. birdseed: What will it be? Who will provide it and how?

_____

_____

"From Bach to the Beatles"

Attention, music lovers. You have two decisions to make: the music for the ceremony and the music for your reception. The selections for both may be similar or each quite different.

First, check with your clergyperson regarding any restrictions that may apply to the ceremony itself. Sometimes, the music is strictly prescribed and you may not have many choices.

If you are allowed to do whatever you please, then you have many choices to consider. A traditional choice is an organist and a soloist playing and singing religious favorites. Another very popular choice is a string quartet playing classical or popular favorites of the bride and groom. Very often friends and family are asked to perform..

Needless to say, it is *never* appropriate for you to sing or play for your own wedding—you are already the center of attention with plenty to do. If you do wish to perform, save it for the reception.

The reception is where you can let loose and be "creative" in your choice of music. Choose from classical or swing tunes, from ethnic folk dances or rock 'n' roll. Invite friends to play, hire bands or quartets, even taped music is acceptable. It all depends on what kind of party you are having.

However, as a word of caution, this letter from an elderly guest may prove helpful since any reception, even the smallest, is likely to include guests of all ages:

> Dear Abby: I'm eighty-seven years old and just back from my granddaughter's wedding. I had a wonderful time except for one small problem, which I wouldn't even mention if my grandson weren't getting married next month. I think I might run into the same situation again and I hope you can help me be polite about this.
>
> The youngsters like to play taped music at their receptions. The music itself is just wonderful but it's too darn loud!
>
> Not only that, but they put those darn speakers up in the front of the room—right beside the tables where us old folks sat. I just hated to, but I had to ask them to turn it down about five or six times!
>
> My question is this: Would I be out of line if I asked them to move my table next time? I have seven grandchildren and this is the second of many weddings to come. I just can't sit through another—I'm afraid I'll lose my hearing.
>
> Also, how long do I have to stay? Even though the bride and groom

left by eleven, I heard that the party went until two o'clock in the morning! I felt bad about leaving at midnight.

> Grandma H.,
> A Reluctant Party Pooper

Dear Grandma: I think your family would appreciate it if you make the suggestion that the speakers be set a distance from the front tables—and closer to the younger folks.

As for when it is appropriate to leave a wedding party, the rule holds that immediately upon the bride and groom's exit from the reception, any guest is free to leave.

♥

Wedding Music Checklist

1. Decide on the mood and type of music you want:
   Ceremony: Consider what you want and *if* you want music for the prelude, solos, procession, recession, etc. List your ideas.
   Reception: Here, too, think about the types of music and *if* you want musical fanfares to announce the receiving line, arrival of bridal party, first dance, cake cutting, tossing of the bouquet and garter, and the departure of the bride and groom. List your choices:

   _____

   _____

2. Select and hire musicians:
   Ceremony: Check with the clergyperson performing your ceremony for guidelines or restrictions.

   Call musicians—Listen to tapes or observe a performance; check availability and any union requirements; set fee; list name and phone number here; notify clergyperson of choice.

   _____

   _____

Reception: Check requirements with person in charge of reception and location for any special rules.

Select and book musicians after discussing the type of music desired, setting fee, checking on union rules; list name and phone number here; notify the person in charge of reception/location.

Note: If you are dealing with an agency or a bandleader who books many musicians, ask for a list of the *specific* players and band leader who will be playing for your event—don't hesitate to ask for an audition or a tape of their playing. Be sure that the specific musicians and band leader names are written into your contract.

Plan the sequence and selection of music for your reception and discuss every detail fully with the leader of the musical group no later than one month before your wedding date. List your musical choices here:

_____

_____

_____

_____

_____

Taped music—List person in charge of selections, taping, and set up. If this is a friend, discuss all details *twice*—one month before the wedding and, again, one week beforehand.

Is the speaker system adequate? Check to see that the speakers will not be set too close to the guests, especially older people. List musical choices here:

_____

_____

_____

_____

_____

Everything decided on? Just one reminder from my mailbag—about the care and feeding of these musical folk be they friends, relatives, or pros:

> Dear Abby: Will you please tell your readers who are planning a wedding reception or a big party with live music to invite the musicians to eat?
>
> Traveling to the job, setting up, and playing from six to eight hours is hard work, and we musicians get hungry. But we never eat our clients' food unless we're invited to, and brown-bagging it is considered tacky.
>
> Sacramento Musician

> Dear Musician: Request honored. And one more tip. If you're asking a friend or acquaintance to perform at your wedding, never assume that their services are gratis. State up-front what you're willing to pay them and give them the option of turning down the fee. And may you never play to a full house on an empty stomach.

Memories Are Made of These. . . .

Your wedding photos, whether formal or candid, become one of your most prized possessions. This does not mean you have to spend a fortune or have thousands of pictures, but you do need to give careful thought to these lovely visual memories.

I urge that you have only professional photographers take both the formal portraits *and* the candid shots at your wedding and reception.

Many brides have been disappointed with the photos shot by friends or family members who meant well, but were unfamiliar with the proper lighting, the right angles, or how to make your favorite people look their very best.

Begin the selection process by asking for recommendations from friends or others who have been married recently and were pleased with their wedding pictures. Ask to see some of their photos before you contact the photographer. The more pictures you examine, the more you will know about the different photographic styles from which you may choose.

Then, select two or three photographers whose work appeals to you and make an appointment to do the following:

73

1. Examine their portfolio of prints from a variety of weddings so you will have an idea of the full range of the photographer.

2. Ask about their approach to photographing a wedding—when do they prefer to shoot the formal portrait, how do they set up for the wedding ceremony, how do they shoot candids, and for how long, does the photographer bring extra equipment in case something malfunctions?

Is the photographer aware of the guidelines for wedding photos established by the church or clergy? If not, be sure that the photographer checks on this.

3. During this time, you can determine whether or not you think he will understand what you want to be reflected in the photos of your special day. Also, this is a person you will be looking at and reacting to throughout your wedding, so be sure you feel comfortable with him or her so that you can relax.

4. Discuss his fees—are there "packages" that might have different prices depending on the amount of time you plan to keep the photographer busy shooting? How many prints do you get? Keep in mind that you may want one set for yourselves, but others for in-laws or parents, and still other prints for some of the people in your wedding party. How much will all these cost?

5. Arrange the dates as soon as possible. The best wedding photographers are usually booked very far in advance.

Video?

An increasing number of couples are having their ceremonies—even their receptions—preserved on videotape. One photographer told me that over half of his studio business is now videotaping special events such as weddings and christenings.

If you are interested in video for your wedding be sure to consider the following:

1. Is video *allowed* at your ceremony? Some clergypeople object to the intrusive cameras. You will need to have the use of video approved beforehand.

2. Use a professional—hobbyists have cameras that may be perfect for family gatherings, but a wedding poses special problems with lighting, sound, and distance that require professional equipment. You *must*

have an experienced person behind the camera. Struggling to watch a shaky, uncomposed picture is no fun. And how disappointing it will be if some of the *right* moments are missed!

3. Ask to see samples of other weddings they have videotaped and check for quality by judging the accuracy of the color as well as the sharpness and steadiness of the pictures.

Remember, everyone hopes to be married only *once*, and during your wedding you have only *one* chance to be sure that your photos capture those magic moments!

Divorce and the Camera

Many young couples have parents and future in-laws who have been divorced or are separated. Thoughtful attention to etiquette is required so that everyone feels comfortable and *included* in the family portraits.

If this is the situation in your family, consider these guidelines:

First, the bride and groom make the final decision. I urge all parents and stepparents to set aside their hurt or anger for this one day and follow the wishes of the bridal pair.

Second, the bridal couple should be considerate of all family members. If you want a photo with your natural parents together, you may also want a picture with each of your parents' new families, too.

Your photos can become a source of fond memories for *all* the people who love you. Be aware of bitter feelings *you* may have—and set them aside.

This is one time during your wedding that you may unwittingly hurt someone's feelings. I know because I receive numerous letters about it. My advice is not always appreciated, as you will see in the following letter, giving special attention to the one that follows it:

Dear Abby: You were wrong, wrong, wrong to tell that woman who is about to marry a divorced man to "grin and bear it" when her fiancé takes her to his daughter's wedding, and is asked to stand next to his ex-wife so his daughter can have a picture of her parents together. Abby, they are not together anymore, and the daughter had better live in the present and forget the past.

The man I married was married before. He has two daughters in their teens, and when they marry, I do not intend to stand by and let my husband take a picture with his "ex" and children to preserve the illusion of a "family." They are no longer a family. As the wife of the father of the bride, *I* should be in the picture—not the ex.

Burned Up in New Castle,
Pennsylvania

Please simmer down and read on:

Dear Abby: A letter in your column struck a nerve with me. I was twelve when my parents' marriage ended in a bitter divorce. When I married at nineteen, my mother had remarried and my father was soon to wed. My wedding went smoothly. I did not seat my divorced parents together. Neither did I expect them to dance together. All I asked them to do was to stand together for one picture with me and my new husband. I didn't do it to "preserve the illusion" of Mom and Dad together. It was my gift to me as a grown woman standing next to her parents.

There is no right or wrong way to handle your wedding photos while trying to adapt to all the ill feelings that usually result from divorce. Be considerate of all parties.

♥

Wedding Photo Checklist

1. Find, consult, and book photographer and/or video camera person. Record names, phone numbers here:

_____

_____

_____

_____

_____

2. Decide on fees. Record here:

_____

_____

_____

_____

_____

3. Set date for wedding portrait. Discuss with the photographer everything you will need for that session, ranging from clothes to cosmetics, etc. List here:

_____

_____

_____

_____

_____

4. Arrange for portrait photo and written description of wedding to be submitted to local and out-of-town newspapers if you are natives of other cities and want your hometown papers to publish details of your wedding. Check with newspaper for date by which this must be received. Record date and name of editor to whom it should be sent.

_____

_____

_____

_____

_____

5. Set time for another consultation one week before wedding to review list of desired shots and to acquaint the photographer with relatives or guests that you want to be sure are included in the photos. Record date here:

_____

_____

As you plan the photography for the wedding day, I strongly recommend the following:

• Have your group wedding photos shot two hours prior to the ceremony so that your entire wedding party—that is, your trip from the ceremony to the reception—is not held up by an hour or more of photos.

• Select a good friend or two who will be happy to serve intermittently as "guides" for the photographer—alerting him or her to good opportunities for candid shots, being sure they know who everyone is, and that your closest friends and relatives are photographed. Choose friend(s) and record names and numbers here:

_____

_____

• Decide *what* you want to be photographed, such as photos before the ceremony of the bride and groom or others; photos during the ceremony (entering, leaving, the kiss, in the car, of wedding party, etc.); photos before the reception (in addition to family group shots); photos at the reception (the cake, musicians, an outside shot of the location, etc.). Be sure to give the friend who will be helping the photographer a "don't miss" list with people and moments specified. Jot your ideas down here:

_____

_____

_____

_____

• Alert your photographer to your special needs on the part of you or your guests. For example:

Dear Abby: I am planning my wedding and have engaged a photographer to take pictures. My problem is that I am blind in my right eye. I have no control over the movement—the eye "floats."
How can I take a nice wedding picture?

August Bride

Dear Bride: Tell the photographer about your problem. It's possible for him to shoot the picture at an angle that will not show your floating eye.

In this case, the bride had the problem. Most of us have one or more family members or friends who would also appreciate special consideration.

"Eat, Drink, and Make Merry"

A real opportunity to imprint your own style! How you entertain your guests reflects who you are as a new couple.

Are you a casual, informal pair that thoroughly enjoys "pot luck" with best friends and a rollicking evening of rock 'n'roll? Or are you more formal—the type for an intimate sit-down dinner with a string quartet?

Family tradition may influence the way you celebrate—the lilting melodies of Ireland, Israel, Poland. Whatever your nationality, it can inspire everyone to share in time-honored customs. If you've been married before, you may prefer a private fete with only your nearest and dearest joining you.

Plan to Enjoy

However you choose to celebrate, your reception is a time to enjoy yourselves. Most important, then, is to make it a time when you are free from any concern over the logistics—even the tiniest detail.

To ensure that, I recommend three important steps:

Number One: As you determine how much you want to spend,

review the prices for the rental of locations that interest you, the estimates from caterers for the number of guests you would like to have, and the cost of liquor (particularly the champagne of your choice), musicians, etc.

What is most important: Would you prefer to have your location draw the attention? That is, do you want to pay more for a posh country-club setting and serve reasonably priced "substantial" hors d'oeuvres? Or do you want a more expensive sit-down dinner for everyone in an affordable hotel banquet hall? Whatever you want, make the decision early so that you can have exactly what you want, *and plenty of time to plan.*

Number Two: Carefully select your caterer. Many caterers will handle everything for you—food, flowers, rentals, bar, and clean-up. A foolproof method to determine what you want and can afford: Establish your budget, then call two or three caterers and say, "I would like to have a reception for _____ number of people and I plan to spend _____ dollars. What can you do for that price?"

The caterer may have a few more questions such as time, the kind of affair you want, rentals, decorations, etc. The caterer will then get back to you with a menu and reception plan to fit your budget. This gives you an opportunity to get to know the caterers. Give yourself several options from which to choose.

Number Three: If you must limit your budget, you might consider handling the bar set-up yourself. One wedding consultant got into her line of work as a result of being a single parent responsible for the wedding receptions of her daughters. She discovered that handling the bar arrangements herself was a very efficient way to control expenses.

With assistance from each daughter, she hired the bartenders, rented the necessary items such as bar, glasses, etc., and purchased all liquor and champagne. That, however, leads to . . .

Number Four: Find a friend who is willing to take over all the details for the day of the wedding, doing the final check on the arrival of the caterer, rentals, etc. *No bride nor mother of the bride nor mother of the groom* should spend any part of the wedding day working on the wedding itself. The responsibility is too exhausting.

♥

Reception Checklist

1. Select and book your location. Record name of site manager and all necessary information. Check to see if your guests will need a map included in the invitation. If outdoors, prepare for alternate plans in case of rain. (They say, "it's good luck if it rains on your wedding day." I've always wondered who "they" were.)

2a. Select and book your caterer. Choose your menu. Double-check your contract to be sure that you and the caterer are in full agreement about the details, including rentals, service fees, drinks, and clean-up. Do not overlook tips. Are the waiters' gratuities included in the caterer's bill, or are these handled separately? Ask the caterer. Add notes here:

2b. If planning to cater your own wedding with help from family and friends, meet with your "helpers" to decide:
   • Who is in charge? (Be sure to have someone other than the bride, the groom, or any family member taking care of details on *the* day.)
   • List your choices and arrangements for food, drinks, service, location, music, flowers, and—don't forget—the clean-up.
   • Make up a checklist of all items and review it regularly. One week before the wedding, hold another meeting of all the helpers to be sure everyone is clear on all details. List helpers and responsibilities here; add to the Wedding Countdown at the back:

81

_____

_____

_____

_____

_____

3. Select and book other services that may not be handled by the caterer such as rentals, flowers, musicians, bar service, etc. Do you need to tip any of these people?
Record all names and necessary information here:

_____

_____

_____

_____

_____

_____

_____

_____

_____

4. Notify site manager of all plans, including caterer, musicians, florist, and bar service. Be prepared to pay a returnable deposit against any damage that may occur during your reception.

82

5. Double-check on clean-up arrangements:

_____

6. Those who prefer a small reception—such as a breakfast, lunch, or cocktail party—should feel comfortable acting as their own hosts. I encourage you, however, to ask a friend to do the actual serving of drinks and food. Add notes here:

_____

_____

7. Special note: Plan for the refreshments for your wedding party *before* the wedding. Preparations begin early in the day. The hours just before a wedding will be much cheerier if everyone who has been assisting and dressing and rehearsing is offered a light snack. (It will also prevent fainting!) Many couples ask a friend to bring sandwiches and soft drinks. Add notes here:

_____

_____

8. One week prior to your wedding: Call the caterer and anyone else who needs a final guest count.

_____

_____

A Toast to the Bride!

The first toast is offered by the best man to the bride. Following that anyone may toast, although I want to encourage each bride to be sure to toast not only her new husband, but also her parents and her in-laws. It's a wonderful way to thank everyone. During the "toast time" it is also appropriate and fun to read any letters and telegrams that may have been sent to the couple.

83

Wedding Toast Checklist

1. Be sure the best man is aware that he should offer the first toast. He may want to write it in advance.

2. Decide if you will need a microphone during the reception so that all the toasts can be heard.

The Cake

O glorious cake! So special it deserves its own section. Like weddings, which are no longer decreed by tradition, wedding cakes, too, now come in many different shapes and sizes and colors.

The traditional tiered white cake has given way to delicious concoctions of chocolate cake, carrot cake, pound cake—whatever you prefer—decorated with pastel touches on the white icing or fresh flowers!

Some weddings have a "groom's cake," too. This is a dark fruitcake, cut into small pieces and individually boxed, for guests to take home. Wedding lore says the unmarried who sleep with this under their pillow will dream of the person they will marry.

If you have been married before, your cake should be ever so slightly more conservative—that means dispense with a fancy bride and groom on the top tier. It does not mean go short on confection. One bride had her caterer make *three* beautiful French cakes—one chocolate, one lemon, and one fabulous strawberry tart—to celebrate her second marriage!

The cutting of the cake takes place after the bridal party has finished eating. The bride goes to the small cake table. The groom stands to her right, the groomsmen to both sides of them. Using a beribboned silver cake knife, the bride cuts the first piece from the bottom tier—and she and the groom share it—politely offering each other bite-sized morsels. Then the cake is served to the guests. Some family traditions encourage the bride and groom to freeze the top tier to be eaten on their first anniversary.

♥

Wedding Cake Checklist

1. Choose your baker. This may be the person catering the reception or the caterer may recommend one. Don't hesitate to show the baker

some pictures of cakes that appeal to you. Select the kind you prefer. Record the baker's name and phone number here:

_____

_____

2. One month before your wedding, reconfirm the cake plans, the date, and time of arrival. Check, too, who will be accepting the cake and making payment. Are there any special instructions for the handling and cutting of the cake?

3. *Be sure* you have a proper cake knife. It's usually a special silver cake knife that can be used for cakes on birthdays and other family events.

4. If you are an adventurous bride who chooses to bake her own wedding cake, allow plenty of time. Have a back-up plan in the event that yours doesn't pan out.

Yes, receptions are a lot of work. But if you will just plan, plan, plan—and check it all over one more time—you'll have the best party in town!

Wish I could be there . . . Abby

6

Your Paper Trail:
From Guests to Gifts
to Gratitude

Your invitations and thank-you notes tell more about you and your fiancé than you might imagine. Within seconds, the recipient knows exactly what kind of people you are.

In fact, nothing says more about you than your "paper trail." It begins with that first envelope in the mail, extending to your responses to guests and gifts, and ends with your expressions of gratitude.

Your Wedding Stationery

Your invitation should be simple, elegant, and truly an example of "less is more"—and your thank-you notes should be warm, unhurried (but not "chatty"), and they should identify the gift. ("Thank you, Margaret and Sam, for the lovely ice bucket.") Don't buy any of those "one size fits all" thank-you notes. They are tacky!

Use the same style stationery for everything—from your carefully worded, formal invitations (engraved or handwritten) to your thank-you notes. The stationery store of your choice will have someone who can help you select the most appropriate paper, type style, and wording.

I can, however, underscore some basic rules that apply to *all* wedding invitations:

1. Determine the *exact* number of guests to be invited and place your

wedding invitation order so you will receive them in time to address and mail them.

The guest list should be divided equally between the bride and groom. Give special thought to inviting the parents of the members of your bridal party, as well as relatives who will not be able to attend but would treasure the invitation. Do not invite casual acquaintances or coworkers unless you enjoy a personal friendship outside the office.

2. I recommend ordering your invitations at least three months in advance so you will have plenty of time to address the envelopes and receive your responses from your guests.

Please note that *every word* is written out on an invitation—that means no abbreviations. Each guest is addressed with their full name and address, including the words "street" and "avenue."

Send your wedding invitations four to six weeks ahead of time, with the request that each guest "RSVP," (which in French means *répondez s'il vous plaît* and in plain English means "Please let me know whether or not you plan to attend"). Each invitation should include a self-addressed, stamped envelope for the response. *Should you not have a response by two weeks before your wedding date*, telephone those you have not heard from to ask "was your invitation received?"

Some people are careless, others incurable procrastinators, and there are those rare instances when an invitation goes astray. (This occurs rarely, but it has happened.)

Also, if you choose an enclosure card for the RSVP that says simply "Please Reply" and provides space for the names, be prepared for some absentminded folks to write only "We're coming!" or "Sorry, we can't make it!"—with no name attached. To save time and frustration, lightly pencil a number inside the envelope flap for the enclosure card, that matches the guest's name on your list. That gives you an instant reference. That also underscores the vital importance of keeping lists (and copies of lists!) of every detail of your wedding plans.

3. Use the "Wedding Invitation List," which can be found at the end of this chapter. It provides space for a master list on which to record—by number—those to whom invitations have been sent, their responses, and the total number of guests attending the wedding and/or reception. If your guest list is limited for any reason, you may want to send announcements of your wedding, to be mailed as soon after the wedding as possible.

If your guest list numbers more than ninety, I recommend using a separate notebook for both the guest and gift lists. Make copies periodically, and keep them in a safe place where they will not be "lost."

4. Order at least twelve extra invitations for last-minute guests and to keep as mementos.

5. I heartily recommend performing this "clerical" chore together. Grooms should be encouraged to take part in the preparations—hopefully they are planning to be a full-time partner in the marriage!

These rules are for *all* wedding invitations. But if you are like most of us, you will have at least one sticky issue to deal with during this stage of wedding planning, whether it's deciding how to announce your second marriage or naming your divorced parents on an invitation in such a way that no feelings are hurt.

Invitations—The Quirks

My mail is always filled with questions from readers who are convinced their problem is highly unusual if not downright unique. But we're all unique and, believe it or not, our "quirks" are really rather common.

The Small, Informal Wedding

Dear Abby: How should I word my invitation for an intimate, informal gathering of just family and our closest friends?

A personal note directly from the bride or her mother is preferable. If it is a small wedding, a phone call is more appropriate. But the brief note on plain ivory paper should be neatly handwritten in dark ink to say:

Dear Diane and Bob,
Amanda is being married in our home to Jim Maple on Saturday,

89

March 25, at 11:00 A.M. A champagne brunch will follow. We would love to have you join us.

Affectionately,
Michelle

A note like this for an intimate, informal ceremony should be sent at least two weeks before the wedding. In response, your guests may telephone their acceptance or send a brief note in the same style:

Dear Michelle,
We are delighted to have been invited to Amanda and Jim's marriage. We look forward with pleasure to seeing you.

Love,
Diane

Invitation to a Second Marriage

Dear Abby: I am planning my second marriage. It will be a modest wedding, which my fiancé (who is also divorced) and I will be paying for ourselves. Must our parents' names be on our invitations and announcements?

Independent and Proud of It

The answer is no. This is a dilemma encountered by many divorced people and older men and women whose parents may be deceased or will not be involved with wedding plans. It is certainly acceptable for a bride to say:

The honor of your presence
is requested at the marriage of
(or "wedding reception of")
Mrs. Amanda Blake
and
Mr. James Maple
etc.

Once upon a time, etiquette decreed that a divorced woman should not send engraved invitations to her second wedding ceremony. I say, why not? With so many "second-timers," I think that old rule deserves to be discarded.

Listing Divorced Parents on an Invitation

Dear Abby: My parents are divorced. I have been living with my mother, but both my parents and their current spouses are hosting my wedding. How should the invitation be worded?

Confused in Cleveland

You have two options. Generally, all the invitations and announcements are in the name of the parent with whom the bride is living—that's usually the mother. Let's assume, too, that your mother is remarried. Your invitation should read:

> Mrs. Margaret Mason
> requests the honor of your presence
> at the marriage of her daughter
> Amanda (etc.)

However, I prefer a different form, which I recently saw for the first time. The parents of the bride and groom were divorced and remarried. Both families were helping with expenses, although the bridal pair was paying for half of the wedding themselves! They wrote:

> Together with their parents
> Amanda Blake
> and
> James Maple
> request the honor of your presence
> at their marriage
> (etc.)

What a lovely solution to a multifamily enterprise!

Invitation to a Belated Nuptial

Dear Abby: What do you think of this invitation from a three-month-old son who was born out of wedlock:

"John Jay Smith requests the pleasure of your company at an open house to celebrate the marriage of his parents, Richard James Smith

91

and Jane Susan Doe, Saturday, June 15, from 2:30 until 5:30 P.M. at their home," etc., etc.

Seen Everything in St. Paul,
Minnesota

Dear Seen: I think it's unique, courageous, and original.

The Invitation to Avoid!

Dear Abby: I am the divorced mother of two small children. When I married eight years ago, my parents gave me a large, expensive wedding. I am being married again and refuse to let my parents give me another wedding. My fiancé has built a nice little home for us. He is not wealthy, just conservative.

We're getting married in my parents' home with only immediate family members and six couples who are very close friends. After the ceremony, we will all go to a small neighborhood restaurant for dinner. I invited the guests by phone and told them all that they would be paying for their own meals. Everyone seemed to think it was okay.

I am enclosing this letter I just received from one of our "close" friends:

"Dear _____: We regret to inform you that we cannot accept your ill-mannered invitation. To invite people to a wedding and expect them to pay for their own meals afterward shows a definite lack of class, taste, dignity, and pride.

"It is really too bad that you can afford to build a brand-new house, but can't see your way clear to pick up the tab for your wedding guests. You two have some nerve! You are just plain cheap and selfish and ought to be ashamed of yourselves."

Abby, were we wrong to ask our guests to pay for their own meals? And what should we do now?

Second-Time Bride

Dear Bride: I think you went overboard trying to conserve when you asked your guests to pay for their own meals. If it's not too late, please pay for your guests' dinners and economize somewhere else.

P.S. The "close" friends who wrote that letter were unkind. A simple "no" would have sufficed.

Guests

A curious thing about invitations: They generate yet another task— outguessing your guests.

You'll soon see why my mail increases immediately after Christmas. That's right—many are in the midst of planning spring and summer weddings and suddenly, the minute the invitation arrives, small, unexpected problems pop up. But do not panic. Forewarned is forearmed.

How to Avoid Guest Gaffes

First—Guard the Guest List

Keep an up-to-date guest list, which you should have begun when writing your invitations. Your list should now include the name, address, and (when possible), phone number of every guest. Beside each name, check whether or not that guest(s) will attend the wedding, the reception, both events, or only one.

For out-of-towners, it is always wise to record *time* of arrival, *where* they will stay, and *whether* they will need assistance in finding lodging. This way you will know where everyone is. Make notes on these things on your guest list.

This list is vital. You must have it for a final count for the caterer and others helping with your reception. You may find it helpful should a gift lose its card but have a postmark on the wrapping. And you are bound to have at least one guest who will fail to respond and must be tracked down to be sure you have no last-minute "surprises."

♥   ♥ DEAR ABBY RED ALERT ♥   ♥

It is imperative that you do not lose or misplace your "Wedding Invitation list."

Second—Guidelines for the Guest's Guest

Brides and grooms with lots of single friends often encounter problems when trying to accommodate the "significant others," casual dates, children, and assorted friends or family members of invitees.

This can be a major hassle if you aren't prepared. For example:

Dear Abby: I'm so angry I'm ready to explode! I am soon to be married, and I cannot believe the number of people who are bringing guests to my wedding. A great deal of planning went into making up our guest list, keeping in mind both the size of the room and the cost of the affair, and I resent all these extra people, most of whom I don't even know.

Only one person called to ask if he could bring a guest. Abby, this is not a backyard barbecue: It's a formal wedding, for God's sake!

What should a bride do when the dining room for her sit-down wedding dinner accommodates 210, and the response cards indicate that 234 will attend? (Incidentally, the dinners cost seventy dollars a plate.)

Has anyone ever telephoned an invited guest who penciled in a couple of extra guests and said, "I'm sorry, but I can't accommodate your guests"?

I've heard, "There's always room for one more," and I suppose there is—but twenty-four more??? Any suggestions?

Furious on Long Island

Dear Furious: If you're asking for my permission to call those who penciled in extra guests to say, "Sorry, I can't accommodate your guests," you have my permission.

That answer generated a flood of letters, including these comments:

"Abby, Do you know how lonely it is to attend a wedding where the focus is on couples, couples, couples and you are there all by yourself?"

"The next wedding invitation that does not allow me to bring an escort, I will decline and stay home where I feel more comfortable."

"We are two single women who are surprised that the bride would assume that thirty-one single people would jump at the chance to attend a wedding alone. . . . We realize the bride has a limited budget and we sympathize but cannot offer a solution. We must speak out for many singles who resent being discriminated against because they are not married."

Get the picture? Decide from your own guest list what will be more comfortable for your friends. However, I feel that most brides resent a single's presumptuousness in "digging up" a date for an occasion that costs a good deal of money.

The bottom line: If you have a single guest whom you know to be involved with a "significant other," then both names should be on the invitation.

For others, you can make it clear that you are not extending an open invitation to an interested *group* by using the names of the invited guest or guests *only* on the envelope containing the invitation. Anyone who disregards this is breaking the rules of wedding etiquette, and should be discouraged with a firm, "I'm sorry, but we cannot accommodate extra guests, although we do look forward to seeing you. Please understand."

Of course, there are times when even that doesn't work:

> Dear Abby: Are we ever on the spot! I will be married soon, and my fiancé and I are putting on the wedding. We are on a very tight budget so we had to keep the guest list down. In order to do so, we decided that we couldn't include any children.
>
> We addressed our invitations to "Mr. and Mrs." Several relatives, and some close friends, have called and asked why their children were not invited, and we told them quite frankly that we had to keep the cost down.
>
> Well, my fiancé's cousin asked if she could bring her two teenaged daughters and her nine-year-old son if she picks up the tab for them! (They live in town.)
>
> Now what should we do? We really don't want any children.
>
> On the Spot

> Dear On: Tell your fiancé's cousin that since no other children will be attending, you would appreciate it if she did not bring hers.

I recently attended a lovely wedding, carefully planned, and professionally videotaped. At one of the most solemn moments during the ceremony, three different toddlers managed to cry loudly. What a shame that the bride and groom have an expensive videotape in which their most precious moments are inaudible.

The problem of children attending weddings can be so frustrating that I'd like to share this letter from one bride:

> Dear Abby: I read your letter from the bride who had relatives

bringing children to her wedding and I wanted to tell you what we did.

We live in a small town where many people are inclined to bring their kids—I feel like I've seen more babies than brides at some weddings—and I really didn't want that to happen to me.

When we had our invitations engraved, my fiancé and I took the enclosure card for the RSVP, and in the lower right-hand corner, we wrote "No Children Please."

Would you believe no one said a negative word to us about it—and not a child attended our wedding!

Wedded in Peace and Quiet

Third—Be Prepared for the Divorce Dilemma

Dear Abby: My parents were married for more than thirty-five years. They were divorced a year ago. It was an ugly divorce as my father had "someone else."

Although my parents are civil to each other, my mother is still very hurt, and, of course, her family has turned against dad.

I am getting married soon. Is it acceptable for my father to bring his live-in lady to my wedding? He has hinted that he would very much like her on the guest list. I don't want to disappoint my father, but I know it would be hard on my mother.

Anonymously Yours

This problem crops up frequently. Here it is in a "related" version:

Dear Abby: Last week my sister got married. When I got there, I was shocked to discover that my sister and my mother had invited my ex-husband and his live-in girlfriend to the wedding and reception!

I was miserable throughout the wedding and stayed only a few minutes at the reception—where I later learned my ex partied all night.

My family knows how I feel about him. If I'd known he was going to be there, I wouldn't have gone. Am I being overly sensitive, or were my mother and sister insensitive to my feelings?

Hurt

How should this be handled? Consider the degree of bitterness of the divorce. Think first of your family members. Then, as the bride and groom whose wishes come first, decide together what to do. And, please, talk with the parties involved beforehand so there will be no surprises to ruin your wedding.

If one of the divorced people is a good friend, but also the one who should not attend the wedding, call and explain the situation saying, "I really wish you could be with us, but we feel it would be uncomfortable for you and for others. Do something special together at another time."

Fourth—Be Prepared to Be "Whelmed"—As in "Over-" or "Under-"

Dear Abby: I recently announced my engagement. Everywhere I go people congratulate me, then they say, "I'm looking for my invitation." Or they ask the wedding date, and when I tell them, they say, "Oh, great, I can make it!"

I'm furious at myself for not saying something on the spot, but I can't invite the whole blasted community! My parents are retired and can't afford to pay for my wedding, so my fiancé and I are footing the bill on a tight budget.

How should I handle this?

Speechless and Fuming

Dear S. and F.: What's wrong with the truth? Tell them you are planning to have a very small wedding because that's all you can afford.

But this may be the most frustrating problem of all:

Dear Abby: You have had many letters in your column from brides who wonder if people don't know what "RSVP" means. It seems that either people don't know they should respond, or they don't care.

Your answer is always the same: "Those who have not responded to indicate whether they are coming or not, need to be contacted by telephone and asked pointedly, 'Are you coming?' "

Well, that doesn't always work. I know because I just tried it. My daughter was recently married, and I telephoned those who ignored the invitation. Several said, "Oh, I thought you knew that we planned on attending," and others replied, "We are going to try to make it," or "We'll do our best to be there."

So what's a hostess supposed to do? Ours was a catered reception that cost fifty-five dollars per person. I still had ten no-shows.

Frustrated

97

Dear Frustrated: Ask your caterer what the "no-show" average is in your area, as well as "no response but show up anyway" and prepare accordingly.

Now . . . on a happier note. Let's talk about wedding gifts.

Gifts

Opening wedding gifts is like having Christmas everyday! I'm sure I do not have to tell most brides-to-be that the wise woman saves those beautifully wrapped packages that arrive daily in the mail and crowd the table at your reception, so you can open them together and in privacy. These can be some of your most precious, shared moments.

♥ ♥ DEAR ABBY RED ALERT ♥ ♥

As each gift arrives, be sure you immediately list the gift and the giver. I cannot stress too emphatically the importance of keeping the giver's card *with* the gift.

Of Wedding Gifts and Words of Gratitude

One—Use the "Gift List" at the end of this chapter or start a notebook in which you record, by number, each gift as it arrives. Specify the date of arrival, the name and address of the giver, and the date you sent your thank-you note. These notes should be sent just as promptly as possible.

I recommend taping a number on the gift to correspond with the number on the list for easy, instant reference.

Two—Write your thank-you notes *immediately* on the note paper that matches your invitations. *Never* use a printed "form" note, not even a card that says "thank-you" on the front.

Take the time to write a warm thank-you, identifying the gift and adding a few personal remarks. It may take a little time and effort, but I promise it will be appreciated.

Who should write the thank-you notes? Both of you. Share the task, or, as an especially nice touch, you might each write a few personal lines to your close friends.

Whatever you do, don't be taken in by anything like the following:

> Dear Abby: I am appalled! I just saw something advertised along with wedding invitations—preprinted thank-you notes for wedding gifts! The message reads: "Thank you for your beautiful wedding gift. It made us very happy and was exactly what we needed." Then the name of the bride and groom is *printed* right on the card!
>
> I am glad to say that I have never received one of those form thank-yous, but since they look so formal and proper, I wonder if some people think they are all right to send?
>
> Will you please comment on the propriety of such cards?
>
> New England Fan

> Dear Fan: A printed, form thank-you note for a wedding gift may "look" proper because it's "formal looking," but the one-message-fits-all thank-you note is in poor taste. It's just one cut above waiting until you run into the giver in person, then giving them a verbal "thank-you."

Three—Give careful thought, *together,* to the gifts you would like to receive. Select just one store at which you will "register" your choices. Be sure to select a broad range of items price-wise so that all budgets can be accommodated. Beyond that, give your family and close friends some suggestions they can pass along to those who are shopping in other towns or cities.

Four—While it is never appropriate to request money, it is wise to select several large items you need so that guests who wish to may contribute toward a joint purchase. Inform your maid of honor and best man of those choices, also anyone else who may be helping you with your plans. This information should be communicated by word-of-mouth *only*.

Five—The bridal couple gives too! Select the gifts *you* will give as early as possible:
- something sentimental and personal for each other;
- for your wedding party, choose any personal memento on which you can engrave the date

Gifts: More Advice and True Tales from Abby's Mail

This chapter would not be complete if I didn't share with you some of the more quotable letters about wedding presents that make opening my daily mail fascinating.

At the same time, I can clarify a few more issues for you regarding wedding gifts, shower gifts, returning gifts, and (at the risk of being repetitious), writing those thank-you notes.

Along with the usual confusion which exists on the subject of gifts for the wedding and/or for the showers, this question surfaces daily in my mail:

Dear Abby: Please settle a disagreement between me and my mother. If a friend or relative is being married and I'm invited to both the bridal shower and the wedding, should I buy one gift or two?

Mother says I should buy one nice gift to be given at the bridal shower. I say buy *two* gifts: a small household item for the shower, and another gift, a more important one, as a wedding gift.

Every time there's a wedding this discussion comes up. We are both loyal readers and agree to let you settle it. If Mother is right, I take her to dinner. And vice versa.

F.C.J. in San Francisco

Dear F.C.J.: 1. You are right.
2. A wedding gift is a wedding gift, and a shower gift is a shower gift, and they're not one and the same.
3. You owe your mother a dinner.

Now, on a similar theme, but new information:

Dear Abby: We received a wedding invitation from a casual acquaintance. What are our obligations? We have never socialized with these people. Must we send a gift even if we decline the invitation? My wife says yes. I disagree. My wife received an invitation to a shower. She declined the invitation. Is it necessary to send a gift anyway? Again, she's not a close friend of the bride or the hostess.

My wife insists that everyone who receives a shower invitation is expected to send a gift whether she attends the shower or not. I submit that no gift is required unless the invitation is accepted.

100

I realize that this is not exactly an earthshaking problem, but if you say I'm right, my wife will have to buy me a lobster dinner.

Philip C. in West Hartford

Dear Philip: Congratulations. You have just won a lobster dinner.

Before we leave the subject of showers and gifts, I want to share a wonderful idea for a shower that is especially appropriate for a bride who is being honored with more than one such event.

Have you ever heard of a Recipe Shower? It's in good taste and doesn't soak the guests. The hostess places two, three-by-five-inch index cards into each invitation and asks the guest to share a favorite recipe. (The extra card is included in case of error or for lengthy recipes.)

At the shower, the hostess presents the bride with an attractive card box to be filled with the recipes contributed by the guests.

Please note this very important fact about wedding gifts: Even though no gift is required, as succinctly stated by Philip in the previous letter, the opposite is also true.

Should a good friend or family member be wed, and you do *not* receive an invitation (perhaps the wedding is a remarriage and, thus, an intimate family-only event), you may want to send a gift. A gift comes from the heart. Some guest lists are limited, especially those for remarriages or couples wanting a quiet, unpretentious wedding. If you send a gift even though you weren't invited to the wedding, what a lovely surprise that will be!

Speaking of surprises—here's one:

Dear Abby: I recently attended a large shower for a young bride-to-be. After the bride opened all the gifts, she passed around some note-sized envelopes and asked every guest to address an envelope to *herself!* I had never seen this done before.

Some girls thought it was practical. Others called it tacky. What do you think?

Wondering

Dear Wondering: I think it's a very clever time-saver. I would not call it tacky.

What *is* tacky? Read on:

101

Dear Abby: What does the mother of an adult (twenty-two-year-old) child do when aforementioned adult child is so remiss about acknowledging important gifts that it becomes embarrassing?

I refer specifically to my daughter who was married last November, and has yet to send thank-you notes for her wedding gifts. (Her excuse: "I've been busy.")

Abby, she was not raised that way; ever since she was a child, I have stressed the importance of sending thank-you notes promptly. Evidently it never got through to her. It's very embarrassing when friends and relatives ask me if "Ellen" ever received their gift. Any suggestions?

Embarrassed Mother

Dear Mother: First, bear in mind you are not responsible for what your daughter does—or does not do.

Some years ago I received a letter from a mother who had the same problem. She enclosed a copy of the letter she had sent to friends and relatives.

Her solution not only got the job done, it made her feel better. The letter:

"Dear Mrs. Murphy: I think six months is long enough for anyone to wait for a thank-you note, so I am taking it upon myself to thank you for the beautiful wedding gift you sent to our daughter. Please accept my apologies for her inexcusable negligence. I assure you, she wasn't raised that way."

Audrey's Mother

I would like to make it plain that I neither approve nor endorse this kind of apology, but I'm sure many a mother will relate to it. However, this daughter resolved that sticky problem herself:

Dear Abby: My husband and I have been married for a while and I have never sent thank-you notes to relatives and friends who gave us wedding gifts. Needless to say, I feel terribly guilty.

Can I, at this late date, send the thank-yous along with an apology? I guess what I'm hoping for is a "magic phrase" that I can incorporate into the notes, which will enable them to forgive me and to understand that I not only want to thank them, but also to correct this seemingly rude omission.

C.H.M. in Braintree, Massachusetts

Dear C.H.M.: The "magic phrase" is: "We are profoundly embarrassed to be writing at this very late date to thank you for the beautiful ice bucket you gave us when we were married.

"Please forgive us for what must seem an inexcusably tardy acknowledgment. Believe us to be terribly ashamed. However, the pleasure we have received from that wonderful ice bucket would warm your heart," etc.

I hope you have kept a list of what each giver gave because if you can make an identifying comment about the gift, you may be more readily forgiven. Good luck.

If a bride or groom must cancel a wedding all gifts should be promptly returned with a note explaining the wedding will not take place:

Dear Abby: My daughter was going to get married, so her friends had a shower for her. Now she's called off the wedding. What do we do with all the gifts? I'd feel foolish giving them back.

Ohio Mother

Dear Mother: Give them back anyway. Whenever a wedding is called off, all gifts should be returned with a handwritten note from the former bride-to-be that simply, briefly explains why.

When it comes to wedding gifts, I probably receive more letters about money than any other type of gift. And no wonder—I saw a magazine article recently that said money is the most popular wedding gift these days. That may be, but handle cash with care. Strict etiquette should be observed when giving or receiving the gift of cash:

Dear Abby: Re: money gifts at weddings: Why not? So many young people live together for a while before they tie the knot and really don't need another toaster or blender.

We gave both of our nephews money for wedding gifts. One of them pooled all his cash gifts and used it for something he really needed—a sizable down payment on a car.

I think the "correct" thing to do in every situation is what is sensible and practical for the people involved.

Any gift given with love and consideration for the recipients is "correct" in my book. Who cares what the etiquette books say!

T.J.F. in Agawam, Massachusetts

Dear T.J.F.: I agree. But the etiquette books say that cash gifts *are* correct. What is *incorrect* is a wedding invitation accompanied by the suggestion that a gift of cash is preferred. In other words, it's proper to *give* cash, but it's not proper to *ask* for it.

And, finally, the odd gift. Everyone receives at least one. An undefinable, usually artsy *objet d'art* only the giver's mother could love. What on earth do you do with it? First, be gracious in your thank-you note. Then, set it aside for a few months—or years.

If you live in a small town, *don't* give it to someone else. Whatever the fate of that unusual gift, take care that *this* doesn't happen to you:

Dear Abby: A reader recently wrote to you about a painting she and her husband had received as a wedding gift from "Andy," a coworker who was an artist. She said the painting was not to their taste, and asked whether she should return it to Andy or hide it in a closet.

I can relate to that because in 1956 I gave a job to an unemployed, needy artist. To show his appreciation, he delivered to my New York apartment some boxes of his artwork as a gift. Unfortunately, they were not to my taste, so rather than hide them away, I returned them, explaining that although they were not for me, I was sure that other people would appreciate them.

The artist understood and thanked me sincerely for not hiding his work in some dark closet.

And so today, the walls of my Encino home are *not* covered with the works of this artist, whose real name happened to be Andy—Andy Warhol!

Mel Ferber
Encino, California

Dear Mel: I'm sure there is nothing I could say that you haven't already said to yourself.

Often my readers write poignantly of life and love. Here's a letter that embodies the spirit of everything wonderful about love and marriage and marvelous memories:

Dear Abby: I've been married for twenty-two years, and whenever I see something we received as a wedding gift, I think of the giver. I cherish the rolling pin from a young cousin, and the rotary egg beater my late grandmother gave us. You can't put a price tag on memories.

My husband's brother took movies during the ceremony, and in front of the church where family and friends gathered afterward. What a priceless gift! If my life depended on it, I couldn't name the people who gave us money.

My grandmother made fruitcake, and my mother baked our wedding cake, which a neighbor decorated. Family and close friends prepared the refreshments. We didn't have a band. We played taped music on a loudspeaker. . . .

Cherished Memories

Cherished writes so eloquently of gifts received. Yet, here's another view—from a reader who writes of *a giftless wedding*. Although that is not exactly the truth:

Dear Abby: You have often been asked how to word a wedding announcement when the couple wants no gifts.

I just received this announcement from dear friends. Both had lost their mates and now they are married. I thought their reference to gifts was worthy of publication. If you agree, please share it.

Grace Von Koss
Birmingham, Michigan

Dear Grace: I agree . . . Dear readers, consider the following, which was enclosed in Grace's letter. It is, I think, a very special invitation, the perfect finale for this chapter:

Believing that we have found
God's perfect will for our lives
William R. Howe
and
Betty Ann Campbell
wish to announce
their marriage
on Saturday, May 10, 1986
at Ward Presbyterian Church
Livonia, Michigan
We respectfully request
no gifts.
We have everything we need.
Now we have each other.
Who could ask for
anything more?

Your Paper Trail: A Double Checklist

Invitations

1. To prepare your "Invitation List," decide on total number of invitations to be sent, dividing the list equally between the bride's family and the groom's.
2. Choose engraving style and paper for invitations, announcements, and thank-you notes. For informal weddings and remarriages, decide on the wording for your handwritten notes.
3. Place stationery order three months ahead of wedding date—or earlier.
4. Address invitations so they can be mailed four to six weeks prior to the wedding.
5. Carefully record responses.
6. Keep copies of all your lists in a safe place.

Guests

1. Record all addresses, phone numbers, and other details needed on guests attending the wedding. For out-of-towners, you may want to record where they are staying and arrival times.
2. Be sure someone is available to help any guests with special needs. This may include handicapped guests or those arriving with small children.
3. Two to three weeks before the wedding, arrange for all those who have not RSVP'd to be contacted by phone for a final confirmation of whether or not they will attend.

Gifts

1. Prepare a "Gift List" on which you will record a description of each gift, the date it arrived, and the date you sent a thank-you.
2. Immediately upon its arrival, tape a number that matches the number on the "gift list" to the bottom of every gift.
3. Write and send your thank-you notes as promptly as possible.
4. Arrange for someone to collect and store the gifts brought to the reception for you to open later.

5. Some brides display their gifts, and some do not. It's a matter of personal choice. For obvious reasons (comparisons will be made), do not display the card with the gift.

P.S. Should you receive a truly unusual gift, then please drop me a note for my next edition. I love surprises!

Happy unwrapping,
Abby

Wedding Invitation List

Name	Address/Telephone	Ceremony	Reception	Notes
		☐	☐	
		☐	☐	
		☐	☐	
		☐	☐	
		☐	☐	
		☐	☐	
		☐	☐	
		☐	☐	
		☐	☐	
		☐	☐	
		☐	☐	
		☐	☐	
		☐	☐	
		☐	☐	
		☐	☐	
		☐	☐	
		☐	☐	
		☐	☐	

Wedding Invitation List

Name	Address/Telephone	Ceremony	Reception	Notes
_____	_____	☐	☐	_____
_____	_____	☐	☐	_____
_____	_____	☐	☐	_____
_____	_____	☐	☐	_____
_____	_____	☐	☐	_____
_____	_____	☐	☐	_____
_____	_____	☐	☐	_____
_____	_____	☐	☐	_____
_____	_____	☐	☐	_____
_____	_____	☐	☐	_____
_____	_____	☐	☐	_____
_____	_____	☐	☐	_____
_____	_____	☐	☐	_____
_____	_____	☐	☐	_____
_____	_____	☐	☐	_____
_____	_____	☐	☐	_____
_____	_____	☐	☐	_____
_____	_____	☐	☐	_____

Wedding Invitation List

Name	Address/Telephone	Ceremony	Reception	Notes
		☐	☐	
		☐	☐	
		☐	☐	
		☐	☐	
		☐	☐	
		☐	☐	
		☐	☐	
		☐	☐	
		☐	☐	
		☐	☐	
		☐	☐	
		☐	☐	
		☐	☐	
		☐	☐	
		☐	☐	
		☐	☐	
		☐	☐	
		☐	☐	

Wedding Invitation List

Name	Address/Telephone	Ceremony	Reception	Notes
_____	_____	☐	☐	____
_____	_____	☐	☐	____
_____	_____	☐	☐	____
_____	_____	☐	☐	____
_____	_____	☐	☐	____
_____	_____	☐	☐	____
_____	_____	☐	☐	____
_____	_____	☐	☐	____
_____	_____	☐	☐	____
_____	_____	☐	☐	____
_____	_____	☐	☐	____
_____	_____	☐	☐	____
_____	_____	☐	☐	____
_____	_____	☐	☐	____
_____	_____	☐	☐	____
_____	_____	☐	☐	____
_____	_____	☐	☐	____
_____	_____	☐	☐	____

Wedding Invitation List

Name	Address/Telephone	Ceremony	Reception	Notes
_____	_____	☐	☐	_____
_____	_____	☐	☐	_____
_____	_____	☐	☐	_____
_____	_____	☐	☐	_____
_____	_____	☐	☐	_____
_____	_____	☐	☐	_____
_____	_____	☐	☐	_____
_____	_____	☐	☐	_____
_____	_____	☐	☐	_____
_____	_____	☐	☐	_____
_____	_____	☐	☐	_____
_____	_____	☐	☐	_____
_____	_____	☐	☐	_____
_____	_____	☐	☐	_____
_____	_____	☐	☐	_____
_____	_____	☐	☐	_____
_____	_____	☐	☐	_____
_____	_____	☐	☐	_____
_____	_____	☐	☐	_____

Gift List

Name of Giver	Description	Thank-you Sent	Date
_____	_____	☐	_____
_____	_____	☐	_____
_____	_____	☐	_____
_____	_____	☐	_____
_____	_____	☐	_____
_____	_____	☐	_____
_____	_____	☐	_____
_____	_____	☐	_____
_____	_____	☐	_____
_____	_____	☐	_____
_____	_____	☐	_____
_____	_____	☐	_____
_____	_____	☐	_____
_____	_____	☐	_____
_____	_____	☐	_____
_____	_____	☐	_____
_____	_____	☐	_____
_____	_____	☐	_____

Gift List

Name of Giver	Description	Thank-you Sent	Date
		☐	
		☐	
		☐	
		☐	
		☐	
		☐	
		☐	
		☐	
		☐	
		☐	
		☐	
		☐	
		☐	
		☐	
		☐	
		☐	
		☐	
		☐	

Gift List

Name of Giver	Description	Thank-you Sent	Date
		☐	
		☐	
		☐	
		☐	
		☐	
		☐	
		☐	
		☐	
		☐	
		☐	
		☐	
		☐	
		☐	
		☐	
		☐	
		☐	
		☐	
		☐	

Gift List

Name of Giver	Description	Thank-you Sent	Date
_____	_____	☐	_____
_____	_____	☐	_____
_____	_____	☐	_____
_____	_____	☐	_____
_____	_____	☐	_____
_____	_____	☐	_____
_____	_____	☐	_____
_____	_____	☐	_____
_____	_____	☐	_____
_____	_____	☐	_____
_____	_____	☐	_____
_____	_____	☐	_____
_____	_____	☐	_____
_____	_____	☐	_____
_____	_____	☐	_____
_____	_____	☐	_____
_____	_____	☐	_____
_____	_____	☐	_____

Special Memories

Did you receive a gift or two that you don't ever want to forget? Why not write a few notes about them here?

The moments between the two of you as you open your gifts may be some of the most precious memories you will have from the wedding. Jot down those thoughts that will be sure to bring a laugh or a tear years from now.

_____

_____

_____

_____

_____

_____

_____

_____

_____

_____

_____

_____

_____

_____

Special Memories

_____

_____

_____

_____

_____

_____

_____

_____

_____

_____

_____

_____

_____

_____

_____

_____

_____

7

Party, Party, Party... People, People, People... Another Planning Challenge

Yes. There are three definitions for the word "party" when you are talking weddings. Even an intimate, at-home nuptial involves more than just you two.

First, you have your "wedding party," by that I mean your maid of honor, best man, bridesmaids, groomsmen, etc. Then you have your pre-wedding events such as showers, rehearsal dinner, groom's party, etc. And, last but not least, that party for two heralded as "the honeymoon."

Careful planning makes the difference between calm and chaos. Think of this as just another stage in your long-range wedding planning—this one devoted to "people management."

Choosing Your Wedding Party

Key Executives—The Best Man and Maid of Honor

The person you choose may be either a family member or close friend—but whoever you choose, select an individual you are confident can do the job *competently.*

For a best man and maid of honor select people who are energetic, responsible, attentive to detail, and enthusiastic about taking on responsibility.

119

These roles demand a lot of hard work. Use the following information as a guide for drawing up a list of duties for each of your chosen "honor attendants."

The Best Man

1. He's the groom's "administrative assistant" and sees that everything is attended to, from checking every detail of the groomsmen's instructions to arranging transportation for the bridal couple's departure from the reception.

2. Helps the groom arrange the "groom's party" if one is planned.

3. Makes sure all the groomsmen are completely outfitted for the big day, including their boutonnieres. He may be asked to double-check on the delivery time of the bridal bouquet.

4. Coordinates all the transportation for the bridal party and the parents at the direction of whoever made the arrangements.

5. Makes sure the groom is carrying the wedding license in his inside pocket and witnesses the signing of the marriage license.

6. Carries the wedding ring or (rings) in his pocket, being sure to remove them from the box beforehand.

7. Takes care of all fees or "donations" made to the clergyman, the church, and other attendants with separate envelopes for each. The groom provides these and any other instructions.

8. Directs the ushers, making sure everyone arrives one hour before the ceremony, knows the locations of telephones, restrooms, cars, keys, the aisle runner, and anything else likely to be needed.

9. After escorting the maid of honor in the procession, he stands to the side of the groom during the ceremony, ready to catch him if he faints.

10. Immediately following the ceremony, the best man checks details for the reception. Once again, he makes sure there is a car for everyone in the wedding party—and that *no one rides with the bride and groom*.

11. At the reception, he is seated at the bride's right and offers the first toast to the married couple, then reads telegrams and serves as master of ceremony for the reception.

12. Finally, he takes charge of the couple's luggage, car and keys, or taxi—and assists them in making their getaway.

The Maid or Matron of Honor

1. Is the bride's "administrative assistant" and oversees all the details of the wedding.

2. Double-checks the bride's complete wedding ensemble to be sure everything is ready the day before the wedding. Her duties may range from providing safety pins to straightening the bride's train after she has kissed the groom.

♥ ♥ DEAR ABBY RED ALERT ♥ ♥

The maid of honor should have a checklist of everything the bride will wear and check each item *by sight* the day before the wedding.

3. She, too, is one of the witnesses to sign the marriage license.

4. She oversees the instructions given to the bridesmaids and female ushers to be sure they are fully informed, arrive on time, and are properly attired.

5. She checks on the arrival time for the bridesmaids' bouquets and corsages.

6. She holds the bridal bouquet during the ceremony and assists the bride with her veil and train as necessary.

7. Most important, she makes sure that everything runs smoothly, taking care of last minute details so that the bride is calm and relaxed.

♥ ♥ DEAR ABBY RED ALERT ♥ ♥

While some maids of honor may assume the responsibility of being one of the chief organizers of the wedding, I will offer the same suggestion I made for the bride's mother: Find someone else to attend to details the day of the wedding so that any major hassles do not disrupt the ceremony. After all, it is physically impossible to check on the arrival of the wedding cake while walking down the aisle just ahead of the bride.

8. Finally, she helps the bride pack for her honeymoon—and makes sure the right luggage is delivered to the best man for safekeeping.

Middle Managers—Groomsmen, Bridesmaids, and Ushers

First, let me make it perfectly clear that in this new era of "nontraditional" roles—*anyone can usher and anyone can propose a toast*. And so the rest of the bridal party should do as they are told. This will depend on local and religious custom, as well as any innovations the bride and groom have chosen.

Those who will assist as ushers are critical to the success of the ceremony and should arrive an hour early. They will have received instructions at the rehearsal the day before, and should be carefully followed.

The only difference between male and female ushers is that *he* offers his arm to the female guest, but *she* walks beside the guest with a male guest following. Otherwise, both should be correctly attired, know where phones and restrooms are, fully understand seating instructions, and be prepared to follow any additional directions from the best man.

Production Crew—Guest Book, Readers, etc.

In keeping with new options for ushers, either a man or a woman may be chosen to oversee the guest book at the ceremony and the reception. One may also be chosen to present a "reading" during the ceremony. If you wish to have the latter, it will be wise to ask the best man or maid of honor to double-check the details such as the reader's understanding of *when* to read, *what* to read, whether or not they have the material to be read with them, what they will wear, and where they should be seated during the ceremony.

Wedding Party Warnings

Warning Number One—Give "Top Management" Power

Choosing your wedding party is "people management" at its most challenging because you are dealing with friends and family who may contribute more emotion and less common sense. Since the people you ask to help plan and execute your wedding are critical to the day's success, let's be frank about the "crisis potential" inherent in any wedding.

People forget that what may be the "happiest" day for the bride, may well be one of the most difficult for her mother. Nerves are frayed, tempers are short, and the work load has probably been horrendous.

So much is happening that strict organization is necessary—with *everyone* adhering to it. The mother of the bride has an industrial strength work load with visiting relatives, and other wedding details—she should be relieved of any specific wedding day responsibilities so she, too, can relax and enjoy her place in the sun as "Mother of the Bride."

In order to reinforce the "follow-through authority" of your best man, maid of honor, and anyone else helping to plan your wedding, treat them as an official management team. Meet regularly to discuss not only the details, but any possible misunderstandings, hurt feelings, or a perception that someone's authority is not being respected.

Set up a system for your management to use when there are disagreements over plans. For example, if Mother felt Daughter was "too bossy," the bride might have said, "But I need to have only one boss to avoid confusion. Since Sis has the time, while your schedule is pretty full, is there something you can do that doesn't need follow-through on the day of the wedding?"

Warning Number Two—Plan For "Perfect," Not "Picture-Perfect"

Dear Abby: My fiancé and I plan to be married next June, and I would like to ask my brother and his wife to be honor attendants. My problem is that they are both quite overweight. It's important for me that everything for my wedding be as perfect as possible. Since there is plenty of time until the wedding, I would like to ask them to go on a diet. I know they can do it because they were both thin a few years ago.

How can I make them understand that I am serious about the weight issues without hurting their feelings?

If they refuse to diet, I plan to ask others in their place.

Slim Sister

Dear Slim: I recommend that you ask others in their place right now. To invite your brother and his wife to be your "honor attendants" on the condition that they lose weight is no honor—it's an insult. Are overweight people any less lovable than underweight people? And since you want everything for your wedding to be "perfect," what do you intend to do about your far-from-perfect values?

Well, that letter generated a few responses:

123

Dear Abby: My hat is off to you for the response you gave that woman. . . . I was recently one of ten bridesmaids, some of whom (myself included) weighed more than three hundred pounds.

We all had beautiful matching gowns made either by the bridesmaid herself or a seamstress, and if I may say so, I think we all looked wonderful. Not only does beauty come in all sizes—so does love and romance. The bride weighed over three hundred pounds, too!

A Big Fan in Butler, Pennsylvania

Dear Abby: I was a bridesmaid only once in my life. We were an odd-looking group. The bride was a size twelve; her maid of honor was a fourteen. I was a sixteen. The groom had two sisters—one was a size three, and the other a fifty-two. She had to have her dress made special, as did the flower girl, who wore a chubby eight.

There was never a doubt in the bride's mind about who she wanted in the wedding party—and it didn't matter what size they were.

I missed being a bridesmaid for my cousin because I was too short, too chubby, and my hair was the same color as the bride's. All her bridesmaids had to be tall, thin, and blonde!

You were right, Abby. A wedding isn't a performance; it's a gathering of your nearest and dearest no matter what they look like.

Once a Bridesmaid in Florida

Warning Number Three—Don't Be Judgmental Whichever Side You Are On

Dear Abby: Please settle a problem for me. I am getting married in a couple of months. My future sister-in-law will be six months pregnant at the time of my wedding. I want very much for her to be a bridesmaid, but I am not sure whether it would be in bad taste because of her pregnancy. She's been married for two years, and her husband (my fiancé's brother) will be a groomsman.

I don't see anything wrong with having an obviously pregnant bridesmaid, but I also don't want to offend anyone. What do you think?

Withhold My Name

Dear Withhold: Bad taste? Certainly not. Invite your sister-in-law to be a bridesmaid, and if anyone is "offended," shame on him—or her.

Some letters are more critical—like these:

124

Dear Abby: A very good friend is planning her wedding and has asked me to be her maid of honor. She's planning a church wedding with all the trimmings, including walking down the aisle in a white wedding gown just like a pure and innocent bride, which she is not. She's presently living with her fiancé.

Most who know her are either laughing at her or criticizing her. This is her first marriage and his second. I told her I couldn't participate in a church wedding because I disapproved of her past conduct and also the kind of wedding she's having.

She is now not speaking to me. This bothers me because we have been best friends since childhood. What do I do now?

Perplexed

Dear Perplexed: The fact that you are "bothered" indicates that you may regret your decision. If so, tell your friend.

Perhaps you may not know that a church wedding with all the trimmings is a first-time bride's privilege and is not reserved for virgins only.

Warning Number Four—Children May Be Hazardous to Your Wedding

You may find few wedding professionals who encourage including children in your wedding party. They may be darling to look at, but they have little tolerance for delays, are easily frightened, and tire more quickly than adults. Read and beware:

Dear Abby: May I share some of my personal experiences concerning children in weddings?

A little flower girl (about two-and-a-half years of age) announced loudly, while she was at the altar with the bridal couple and minister, "I have to make a wee wee." (She wasn't lying; she made a puddle during the ceremony.)

The ring bearer, an attractive little boy of three, took the pillow and kept throwing it up in the air and catching it (sometimes) during the entire service. He was seated between his parents and neither one attempted to discipline him.

Frequently, during the procession, the kids do not make it up the aisle, but wander instead to an aunt or an uncle on the way there, and cannot be prodded to go where they went during rehearsal.

Kids crying in the church (or synagogue, or whatever) are an invasion to the sacred ceremony, and well do I remember the words of a minister, "A baby who cries in church is like a New Year's resolution— it ought to be carried out."

A bolder colleague once said, while a baby persisted in crying during the service: "Will that mother with the crying baby please give her a bust in the mouth?"

Now I've said it. Use it as you deem advisable. It is all true.

> The Reverend Paul E. Farrell,
> Ontario, California

Warning Number Five—Keep Your Friends and Break Tradition

Dear Abby: My fiancé and I are planning our wedding for this fall. I know it's customary for the bride to have her closest friend for her maid of honor, but, Abby, my closest and dearest friend happens to be a man. My fiancé doesn't know him very well, but he understands how much this man means to me, and he agrees that he should be part of the wedding party.

He can't be best man because my fiancé's brother is going to be best man, so where would it be appropriate to put my friend in the wedding party?

It will be a church wedding.

> Sincere

Dear Sincere: Your male friend could be an usher or a groomsman, or, instead of "maid" or "matron" of honor, he could be a "man of honor." A bit unconventional perhaps, but it's your wedding and it doesn't hurt to bend the rules to show love and respect for your dearest friend.

Of Processions, Recessions, and Concessions

Every region of the country, every religion, every family has its own traditions. While I defer to clergy and to local customs on matters ranging from the bridal procession to the throwing of the bridal bouquet, I can offer helpful hints on several procedures.

Seating

As the guests arrive for the ceremony, the only basic guideline, for a short time, is bride's family guests to the left, groom's family guests to the right. But once the seats begin to fill, the most important goal is not separation but balance. Humor the guest only until the attendance becomes too weighted in one direction, then seat later arrivals wherever necessary to keep the crowd balanced.

A more delicate question is how to seat the family, especially when confronted with the ubiquitous "divorce dilemma." Here is the usual program:

1. First the paternal, then the maternal, grandparents of each are ushered down to their seats after all the guests have arrived. (Note to best man: Do these folks need a place to sit while waiting to be ushered?)

2. The groom's mother is then escorted to her seat, followed by her husband. Should she be divorced or remarried, she would occupy this seat alone or with her second husband. The groom's father, alone or with his wife, would be seated behind her.

3. Last to enter before the bride is the bride's mother. She is escorted to the first pew on the left where she will be joined by the bride's father after he escorts his daughter. Should she be divorced or remarried, she will occupy this seat alone or with her husband. The bride's father, then, occupies the second or third seat with his wife.

4. Ultimately, if these arrangements do not work for personal reasons, the bride and groom should establish the desired seating with all the individuals involved well before the ceremony and provide the best man with a seating chart.

Dad's Role—Giving the Bride Away

You can imagine the mail I've received on this one!

Dear Abby: I am a fifty-eight-year-old woman. When I was a young girl, I attended a formal wedding and was greatly enraged when I heard the minister ask, "Who gives this woman?"

The question still arouses my anger, and I am amazed that more women are not insulted by this question—asked publicly yet!

Only the woman herself has the right to "give" herself to anyone, any time, for any reason.

I've finally begun to express defiantly my indignation when a bride-to-be tells me she is going to be "given away" by her father or stepfather. Of course, I am a "nut" to even suggest that a woman belongs to no one but herself, and is not an inanimate object to be "given away."

Thanks for listening.

Margaret Jonas in San Francisco

Dear Margaret: The original marriage vows were written during biblical times when a woman was considered "chattel"—a piece of property owned by her father. He had the right to "give" her to her husband, who then regarded her as *his* property.

However, in recent years, many couples have requested that that portion of the marriage ceremony be omitted for the reason you cited.

This letter arrived on the heels of the above:

Dear Abby: This is in response to the feminist who was enraged by the phrase, "Who gives this woman in marriage?"

I always wanted my father to walk me down the aisle, but I never particularly cared for the tradition of being "given away." Although I did not express my feelings about this, after my father walked me down the aisle, and the minister said, "Who gives this woman in marriage," my father said, "With her mother's and my best wishes, she *happily gives herself.*"

By the way, I had a real "family" wedding: My grandfather was the minister, and my grandmother was my matron of honor!

Another variation on the same theme from an older bride:

Dear Abby: I am a fifty-four-year-old single woman. I have never been married and plan to wed a wonderful man I met at work. . . . We are having a small church wedding, but I don't want anyone to "give me away." Is that an essential part of the marriage ceremony? If so, how should I handle it?

Autumn Love

Dear Autumn: It is not imperative that you be "given away." Ask the clergyperson who will officiate at your wedding to omit that portion of the service. The marriage ceremony is not carved in granite. Your wedding can be as creative and comfortable as you want it to be. Just check with the clergyperson to be sure it's legal. Good luck to you and your beloved.

Moms Are People, Too

And, to complete our view of how things have changed over the last twenty years:

Dear Abby: Is there anything "improper" about having the mother of the bride escort her daughter down the aisle?

My father will be a guest at my wedding, but he and my mother have been divorced since I was a small child and my mother raised me alone.

Sentimental

Dear Sentimental: Improper? No way. Discuss this with the clergyperson who will perform the ceremony, and good luck.

Clearly the traditional role of the bride's mother has changed and continues to change. A word of caution for the bride who has a working mother and is considering a large, traditional wedding:

Take time to talk with your mother about your expectations of her, as you may be surprised at the constraints on her time. She may be limited in what she can do. Nor will she appreciate "too much direction" in certain areas. Today's working mother is an independent person, like you. I know because more and more often I receive letters like this:

Dear Abby: I feel so guilty. I am a working mother whose twenty-two-year-old daughter is insisting on a huge traditional wedding. Both her father and I would prefer she put the ceremony off, live with her fiancé for a couple years to be sure they are right for each other, and forgo all this expensive hullabaloo.

She will have nothing to do with that.

Also, she tried to tell me what color dress to wear and I told her I'd wear what I feel good in, whatever color it may be.

People keep asking me if I'm enjoying "this exciting, wonderful time." My answer is no, no, no. I think that these expectations of how the bride's mother is supposed to act and feel are totally out of line with today's world. I can't put my job and my whole life aside just to

129

plan a wedding for the next year. Is there something wrong with me?
A Too-Modern Mother

Dear Mother: No, you are reacting like any hardworking contemporary mom. If your daughter wants a wedding with all the trimmings, then it's her responsibility to arrange it. The fact that her parents are willing to pay the bill is more than enough, in fact more than most parents can afford even when both are working!

Be up-front about your feelings. If your daughter is ready to wed, then she's ready for reality.

Time Out for Treats

A word of caution: Everyone in your wedding party will be doing their best to be on time, practice, and perform correctly. This takes hours, both at the rehearsal and throughout the wedding day itself. To prevent crabbiness and fatigue, especially for the bride and groom and their honor attendants, plan to take time out for sodas and sandwiches. Make it a surprise and everyone will step happily down the aisle.

The Receiving Line

Whether you "receive" at the door of the church following the ceremony, or at the reception—immediately following the formal photographs (which I have already recommended be done *before* the ceremony so there is not a two to three hour tedious wait for guests)—the line-up can be flexible.

It used to be that both the mothers headed up this reception line with fathers not even appearing. However, most dads today, like their sons, enjoy a higher profile at the wedding, and I think *everyone* should be included.

One line-up that I heartily endorse starts with the mother of the bride, followed by the father of the groom, the bride, the groom, the mother of the groom, and the father of the bride. If this is the bride's second marriage, only the bride and groom "receive."

Now—if parents have been divorced or remarried—you have several options, including doing it in a way that will make everyone feel most comfortable. Some choices:

1. Have the natural parents take their places in the line as suggested above, and their new spouses attend the reception as guests.

130

2. If the bride's mother contributes financially to the ceremony and her father to the reception, then the father should head up the receiving line and his new spouse take a place in the line, too. The bride's mother will have had her turn in the front pew during the ceremony.

3. Often, however, the bride lives with her mother and may want her mother to head up the receiving line with her new spouse. That is perfectly acceptable.

As you can well imagine, the receiving line for families with divorced parents can become an emotionally charged element of wedding planning. It has been the source of one of my few boo-boos:

Dear Abby: My son was married recently. His father and I are divorced and his father is remarried.

My question: Should my ex-husband's wife have been in the receiving line? If so, where should she have been standing?

Abby, she stood in the receiving line beside the bride, and I had to stand at the very end.

Please answer in the paper. I want to show it around.

Mother of the Groom

Dear Mother: Somebody goofed. She should not have been in the receiving line at all.

My answer ran on January 24, 1985. By March 20, I had to answer to my readers!

Dear Abby: Your answer to "Mother of the Groom" was totally off-base . . . in some cases a stepparent most certainly should be in the receiving line. Some stepparents play an important role in the step-child's life.

Questions such as "How long has the stepfather been remarried?" and "With whom do the children live?" were not answered in the letter. The relationship between the stepparent and the child or his or her new spouse must also be considered.

It's their wedding, and they should have a say in the matter.

Stepparent-to-be

Dear Stepparent-to-be: I agree, the circumstances can make all the difference in the world. In this case, for brevity's sake I omitted some facts from the published letter, such as the bitterness of the divorce since the groom's father had a girlfriend waiting in the wings.

131

Many readers wrote to complain about my answer—they were right.

However you decide, discuss the matter forthrightly with everyone involved and make your decision on what works best—in your family's situation—to make the day a happy one. When confusion reigns, do it the way the bride and groom want it.

Getting everyone in the right spot is the hard part, now just keep it moving and remember that, etiquette-wise, guests should not eat or drink before going through the receiving line. So make it snappy!

Of Pre-Parties and Post-Parties

Nothing provides a better excuse to party out than a wedding. From showers to bachelor events to the rehearsal dinner, it can seem like one endless bash. The secret to enjoying each is, of course, planning. A few words about each event, what to expect, and how to manage each.

Showers

No more than one or two should be given for you, and then only by close friends or *distant* relatives, never by an immediate family member. Also, people should not be invited to more than one shower, so vary the guest list for each party. Expect small gifts—practical items that don't tax the pocketbooks of guests, who are also expected to shell out for a separate wedding present.

Be aware of the following "party perils" that people have written to me about:

> Dear Abby: I'm having a bridal shower for my daughter who is getting married. Must I invite all the people I am having at the shower to the wedding, too?
> My sister says that everyone coming to the shower must be invited to the wedding, too. I say, "Not so!" What do you say?
> The Bride's Mother

> Dear Mother: It's true. Score: sister: 1, you: 0.
> And by the way, Mom, bridal showers should not be given by close family members. Friends, aunts, cousins, *si*. Mothers, *no*!

Beware of overprogramming:

132

Dear Abby: We recently attended a wedding in another state. On the day before the wedding, there were two bridal showers for out-of-town guests.

Tell us, Abby, is this proper etiquette? And what do you think of that idea?

"Us" is Greenville, South Carolina

Dear "Us": It is not proper etiquette. I think the showers were intended to soak the wedding guests.

As usual—the divorce dilemma:

Dear Abby: This is my first Dear Abby letter, and it's written because I am hurting. To promote good feelings, I volunteered to give a bridal shower for my stepson's fiancée. (I'll call her Marcy.) I had two invitations left over, so I gave them to Marcy for her bridal scrapbook.

Later, I received a telephone call from my husband's first wife thanking me for the shower invitation! I told her that I had not invited her, and didn't know who did. She came anyway.

When I confronted Marcy, she explained that in her family it is traditional to always invite the groom's mother!

Abby, I have never heard of Wife Number Two being asked to entertain Wife Number One. I feel betrayed, angry, and hurt, and although I played the perfect hostess during the shower, I am still angry.

Wife Number Two

Dear Wife Number Two: Marcy may have meant well, but she had no business inviting anyone to the shower without your permission. But be charitable. The bride-to-be may have been more naive than malicious.

Wife Number One used very poor judgment in attending the shower after being bluntly told by you, the hostess, that you had not invited her.

Now, give yourself a break and put aside your anger. You will harm only yourself by nurturing it.

Bachelor and Bachelorette Events

Once again, my readers say it better:

Dear Abby: I'm twenty-three and have been dating the same man for eight years. We have decided to get married soon. The problem: My fiancé has a group of buddies—most of them he has grown up with and they are very close. When one of these buddies gets married, they have a traditional bachelor party, including strippers.

I don't approve of this at all and asked my fiancé how he felt about it, and he said he didn't care for that sort of thing either. When he told the organizer of this party that he didn't want strippers at the stag, he was told it wasn't up to him, it was up to the guys giving the party, and they wanted strippers.

One of the wives said it was no big deal, but I disagree. What's the solution?

Prude

Dear Prude: Your fiancé should inform his buddies that if they insist on having strippers, knowing how strongly he feels about it, they should not be surprised if he skips out when the strippers shimmy in.

Then, get a load of this:

Dear Abby: My best friend, "Denny," was engaged to be married three months ago, so I threw a stag party for him that turned out to be a big mistake.

I hired "Salome," an exotic dancer, to entertain at this party the night before the wedding, and Denny ended up in bed with her. To make a long story short, Denny's fiancée heard about it and called off the wedding.

Now Denny is making plans to marry Salome. My question: Should I give Denny another stag party?

Lester

Dear Lester: I vote no, but if you do, don't hire another exotic dancer. Ask Salome to dance—and retain the seventh veil for her wedding.

Another party idea worth mentioning was sent by a reader—this one *I* endorse:

Dear Abby: I was just married and something unusual happened that I thought might solve the "stag party problem" for your readers who are always complaining about strippers, etc.

Several months before our wedding, our best man and maid of

134

honor asked us if we would consider a "Jack and Jill Party." They would plan it, everyone in our wedding party would participate, and we would forgo the traditional bachelor party and showers.

It sounded great and it was! We selected a date two weeks before the wedding. The best man and maid of honor rented the Eagles hall, put one groomsman in charge of the bar, one bridesmaid in charge of food, hired a band, and sent out invitations.

Included on the invitation was a request for five dollars a person, which paid for the party (the food was potluck) and went toward one large gift (a VCR!).

Everyone had a great time. Over two hundred people attended and we danced our hearts out.

"Jill"

Dear Jill: Thanks for a great idea. I'll pass it along.

Of Memorable Nights and Marvelous Mornings

That's what honeymoons are made of. But, in addition to planning, think "pooped." That's what you'll be by the end of your wedding day. So, do plan ahead for smooth sailing, but let me share with you one reader's advice that might save the day:

Dear Abby: My sister and I were recently wed in a double-ring ceremony. I'm doing great and she's already thinking about a divorce.

Why? She had a miserable time on her honeymoon. I don't think it was her husband's fault—they both put planning it off until the last minute, and then the night after our wedding all their reservations fell through, they had a big fight, and they're still barely speaking.

Meanwhile, my husband and I did something that everyone thought was pretty silly, but we had the best time!

First, we checked into a local hotel and changed into jeans and sweats. Then, we went to McDonald's for a snack and to the late movie—a comedy. By the time we got back to the hotel, we were exhausted but relaxed. We slept late the next morning, talked to our folks to say "thanks" for everything, and caught a late afternoon flight. Our honeymoon was just a week long because we both work, but it was perfect.

Don't you think our way might have made a big difference?

Blissed Out

135

More couples should be aware that the bigger, more elaborate the wedding, the more likely they will be so tired that honeymoon expectations should be realistic. Take it easy!

By the way, "Blissed Out" made a gracious gesture that should not go unnoticed: The new couple took time out from their special time together to call and thank their parents. If you have folks who are putting time and/or dollars into your wedding, please put it on your list to do the same. What a lovely way to end your big day!

♥

Wedding Party Checklist

1. List those you would like to have in your wedding party.

_____	_____
_____	_____
_____	_____
_____	_____
_____	_____
_____	_____
_____	_____
_____	_____
_____	_____
_____	_____
_____	_____
_____	_____

2. Write down what it will cost each, how far they will have to travel, and how much time it will involve.

_____

_____

_____

_____

_____

_____

_____

_____

_____

_____

_____

_____

_____

_____

_____

_____

3. Call the people on your list, discuss the details with them, and see if they can afford—dollar-wise and time-wise—to be in your wedding. List their names, addresses, and phone numbers here as they accept.

_____

_____

_____

_____

_____

_____

_____

_____

_____

_____

_____

_____

_____

_____

_____

_____

_____

4. Meet with your best man and maid of honor to make a list of duties for each that includes key responsibilities for helping the bride and groom, directing the bridesmaids and groomsmen, preparing seating charts, checking on clothing, rings, marriage license, flowers, cars, and their assistance with reception events such as toasts, collecting and storing gifts, cutting the cake, tossing the garter and the bridal bouquet, and exiting the reception.

Set dates to go over each list with the individuals on a regular basis. Add this to your Wedding Countdown. List here what each will take responsibility for:

5. One month, and again one week before the wedding, double-check these lists.
6. Stay in touch with your best man and maid of honor on any "management" issues of an emotional nature that may need handling. Do the same with others in your "top management team," so you can spot trouble before it happens.
7. Draw up seating charts for rehearsal dinner, ceremony, and the receiving line. Discuss this with everyone in the wedding party so all are in agreement. Keep copies of the seating charts available for review.
8. Record the dates for all parties to be given for you. Respond immediately afterwards with thank-you notes for shower gifts—and a thank-you note to the host or hostess. Please check the guest lists for each party so that a different group is invited to each.
9. Three months (or earlier) before your wedding, make plans for your honeymoon and purchase plane tickets. Please note that transportation to popular spots such as Hawaii or Bermuda can be difficult to get at the last minute. Will you need passports or visas? Add the dates for finalizing these plans to your Wedding Countdown.
10. Sometime during the weeks just before or just after your wedding, set a date for your "Second Honeymoon."

Now have a wonderful time!

Abby

8

"And the Bride Wore Black!"

You don't believe me? Check it out:

Dear Abby: My problem may seem rather odd, and you'll probably think I'm weird, but here goes: I am going to be married soon and I have already designed my wedding gown and plan to make it myself. It's going to be black lace and taffeta. I've told only a few people and have already been ridiculed, asked if I was "crazy," and I was even accused of being a Satan worshipper. I am not. I believe in God, I just happen to like black.

I know from history that white was not always the traditional color for brides. In our culture black is worn by mourners, but I am not superstitious. In other cultures, white is worn for mourning, so why not black for weddings?

I have had only one positive reaction from a friend who heard I was going to be married in black. She said, "It figures. You always were different."

I would appreciate your opinion.

Different in Indiana

Dear Different: What does your fiancé think? His is the only opinion you need. If he has no objection, go with the black, and good luck.

That letter—and my answer—illustrate how the rules have changed for today's brides.

Should you think I'm a little weird supporting a bride who wants to wear black, reserve your judgment. Here's a second opinion from a wedding expert with impeccable credentials:

Dear Abby: I have read with great interest the controversy surrounding white weddings in your column and applaud the encouragement you have given women who see their weddings as a celebration of their faith in the future, not an apology for the past (even if they have been living with their fiancés).

White has been a color of joy since Roman times. Traditionally, ceremonial robes have often been richly colored, whether they were peasant costumes or gold-embroidered kimonos.

During the Middle Ages red was the favored color, and it still is the color chosen by Hindu, Islamic, and Chinese brides.

The white wedding dress is a fairly recent tradition. Victorian brides from privileged backgrounds wore white to indicate that they were rich enough to wear a dress for one day only—but still the majority at that time wore their best finery.

We who now live well into our eighties (as opposed to our fifties in 1900) must also develop a more tolerant view of the needs of people who, like half of all U.S. citizens, will probably divorce and remarry in their lifetime. Their sincere efforts to begin again should be supported by the community they seek to join. In unity there is harmony, and color should not bar the way.

Barbara Tober,
Editor-in-Chief
Bride's Magazine

". . . Women who see their weddings as a celebration of their faith in the future . . ." What a lovely statement and a wise one. With that in mind, a bride should wear whatever she feels will make her absolutely beautiful in her own eyes and the eyes of the man who loves her. So whether your wedding dress is long, short, old, or new, choose the one that's *really you*.

Of course, many brides are making decisions that affect what is worn by others, not just members of the wedding party, but their parents, too. And some brides may be planning a wedding that is not their first. In my book, there are just a few rules of etiquette and guidelines to observe when it comes to proper attire for everyone involved in your wedding.

First, should you plan to have attendants, keep one theme in mind and follow through for a unified look. That doesn't mean you can't combine a formal wedding gown with informal bridesmaid dresses, or a tux for the groom and dark suits for his groomsmen, but it does mean *continuity*. Keep the style of dress the same for all members of your wedding party.

Second, know the cost of the bridesmaid dresses and tuxedo rentals *before* you ask anyone to be in your wedding party. Of course, you want your "nearest and dearest" to be in your wedding party, but you don't want your wedding to force them into hock. And if your best friend already has five never-to-be-worn-again bridesmaid dresses hanging in her closet, please don't add one more.

When choosing your wedding party, it is important to be straightforward: As you ask each friend to be in your wedding, be sure to tell them the cost of the clothing you will ask them to purchase *before* they make their commitment. If they decline your invitation, accept that gracefully without pressing to know "why." (Of course, if you recently won the lottery, you can offer to pay for everything yourself!)

Here's what can happen when there is "miscommunication" on this matter:

Dear Abby: I was married in June of 1987, and if I say so myself, it was the prettiest wedding I've ever seen. The only drawback is that it cost me a fortune.

My folks paid for most of it, but I picked out five bridesmaid dresses at $129.95 each and told my bridesmaids that each would have to pay for her own dress. One girl backed out after her dress got here, and I had to replace her. It wasn't easy because she is a size five and none of my girlfriends could fit into her dress. My fiancé had a thin, twelve-year-old cousin who could wear it, so she filled in.

Anyway, none of the bridesmaids could pay for their dresses at the time, so I charged them to myself and they all promised to pay me back. Well, a whole year has gone by and I haven't seen a dollar from any of them!

I have written them letters and called them on the phone, and all I get is hard-luck stories, so I am sending them each this poem I cut out of a *Dear Abby* column a while back:
I think that I shall never see
The dollar that I loaned to thee;
A dollar that I could have spent
On many forms of merriment.
The one I loaned to you so gladly

145

Is now the one I need so badly.
For whose return I had great hope
Just like an optimistic dope.
For dollars loaned to folks like thee
Are not returned to fools like me.

If you print this, please don't use my name or location. I just want to warn other brides not to be as foolish as I was.

Too Trusting

"Too Trusting" received quite a few letters after hers appeared in my column, including this one:

Dear Abby: What a pity "Too Trusting" didn't make her arrangements earlier! She should have asked her bridesmaids to sign legal contracts in advance, agreeing to pay the $129.95 for their dresses. That way she'd have lost her friends before the wedding, rather than afterward.

If the girls had gone ahead and paid for their dresses, they would have had all the hard feelings—courteously concealed, of course. The bride's smug memories of a perfect wedding wouldn't have been sullied by thoughts of "selfish" friends who refused to cooperate in a ripoff.

The traditional way has lasted for a long time because it has a practical and honest realism about it. The bride and her parents are responsible for the bride's expenses; their financial ability determines how "showy" the ceremony will be. It's the occasion and not the show that counts.

All too often, remembering the "show" brings second thoughts when a couple finds in their new life together that the money could have been spent more wisely. Simple weddings can be beautiful, and there are no friends lost, no regrets about overspending.

One of our daughters had a lovely park wedding; in her invitation she included a map of the location and asked all to share in a potluck celebration dinner after the ceremony. Bride and groom furnished cake and beverage, and over 150 friends showed up with food and gifts galore.

The outdoor setting, a simple arch with flowers and greenery in the background and singers accompanied by a harp, made the occasion memorable. Everyone enjoyed the occasion, including a large group of park users who watched from a distance.

Needless to say, all the memories of this wedding are pleasant and precious.

A Delighted Mother of the Bride

Need I say more? So choose a formal or informal wedding style according to your heart's desire. There was a time when the bride who married for the second time did not wear a wedding gown or veil, but today circumstances determine the "rules."

Times have changed and I've changed with the times. If a big, splashy wedding—with all the kids from your about-to-be blended families—is right for you the second time around, then go for it!

Addressing Those Wedding Dress Doubts

Here's a sample of some typical problems. I think the reason I hear so often from so many is that a recent boom in "traditional" weddings is occurring just as some of the old "traditions" of etiquette are now outdated. My responses to the following should help you through the maze:

Doubt Number One—"What If I Don't Want to Wear My Mother's Wedding Gown?"

Dear Abby: I am twenty-one years old and planning my wedding. I picked out a beautiful satin and lace wedding gown, but here's the problem: My mother wants me to wear the wedding gown *she* wore when she got married.

I hate to hurt her feelings, Abby, but I tried it on, and I don't care for it at all. Maybe it just doesn't look good on me, but I really hate to think of wearing it on my wedding day. It looked good on my mother in her day, but there is no way I could feel beautiful in that wedding gown.

Please, please help me get out of wearing it, Abby. Or should I wear it and keep my mouth shut? My fiancé saw the gown I want to buy (we picked it out together), and he says I should ask you. I would be paying for it with my own money.

September Bride

Dear Bride: Be honest with your mother. It's your day, and I know she wants you to *feel* beautiful. Tell her that you have found the wedding dress of your dreams, and that's what you'd like to wear!

Doubt Number Two— "What If I Can't Afford a New Wedding Gown?"

Dear Abby: My fiancé and I shopped everywhere for a wedding dress and we were really discouraged by the prices. All this money for a dress I will wear once?

Then we opened our newspaper and read about a special sale at a thrift shop where designer wedding dress samples were to be sold for as little as one hundred dollars! The sale was sponsored by Planned Parenthood.

We didn't find anything we liked but it gave us an idea—so we combed the racks at some other thrift shops and voilà! I found it—the perfect dress at a price that didn't bankrupt me. In case anyone thinks this is really tacky—what's tacky about the two of us looking for it together, paying a reasonable amount of money that we both agreed on, and knowing that my fiancé thinks I look really pretty?

Pretty Not Pricey

Another bargain hunter chimes in:

Dear Abby: I saw a letter in your column from the bride who found her dress in a thrift shop. I did, too!

We have five children between us, we both work, and we simply could not afford an expensive wedding. But—here's the kicker—my husband sews! So he made all the alterations on my dress. (He's also sixteen years younger than I am.)

I couldn't imagine a more wonderful wedding day than ours. I *felt* beautiful and that's what counts.

Loved and Lovely

Doubt Number Three— "If the Bride Is Formal, Must the Groom Be, Too?"

Dear Abby: Dudley and I are planning our wedding. It's going to be a formal church wedding and we want it to be perfect in every detail.

We agree on everything with one exception: Dudley hates to wear a necktie.

What do the fashion experts suggest as a compromise?

Dudley's Darling

Dear Darling: The tie that binds in a wedding has nothing to do with what the groom wears around his neck. If Dudley hates neckties because they're uncomfortable, he can leave the top button of his shirt unbuttoned. But the fashion experts say there is no compromise. A man is either formally attired or he isn't.

That's one answer to her question. Here's another: If you assume few "fashion experts" will be attending her wedding (or yours, for that matter), why not allow Dudley to be comfortable in the style he prefers, and have the groomsmen adopt the same style? It's an option and one sure to make your wedding more memorable for your guests. Dare to be different!

Doubt Number Four— "Must the Mothers of the Bride and Groom Wear Mauve?"

Dear Abby: I am furious with my daughter. She is planning her wedding and just called to instruct me that I'm supposed to buy a mauve dress so I won't clash with the bridesmaids or the mother of the groom (whom she is telling to wear gray).

I want a dress that makes me look wonderful, not like part of the window treatment. For heaven's sake, I'm only forty-three years old!

Please tell me the best way to handle this. I'm not going in mauve anything.

Too Young to Be a Dowdy Dowager

Variations of that letter must appear in my mail at least once a week. Why? Mothers have changed—they work, they work-out, they have full lives, today they look younger at forty-five than forty-five looked in the fifties.

So what's a daughter to do?

First, the only style you should set is that of your wedding party— meaning bridesmaids and groomsmen. The day of telling mothers what to wear is past. You should, instead, encourage them to select whatever they feel good in. Unlike wedding gowns, they will want dresses they can wear again and again.

Second, read the following as it holds a lesson for today's bride who may be planning a formal wedding that will be attended by friends and family who lead informal lives:

149

Dear Abby: After seeing all the letters in your column from people who complain about the high cost of being a bride or a bridesmaid—I want to report on a beautiful scene I just witnessed.

The July wedding was formal—at least the bride and groom were formally attired. But the bridesmaids' dresses were outstanding in their design. They were street-length navy blue linen chemises with high V-necklines and a pleated flounce at the hem. The chemise line was elegant on the slender bridesmaids and flattering to the heavier ones. They all wore wide-brimmed straw hats, a simple strand of pearls, and short white gloves. Best of all—that dress will go to the office, to a dinner party, anywhere!

And the mother of the bride wore a dress of a similar design in beige. The groomsmen, unlike the groom in his "tails," wore dark business suits. They looked so tailored and classy.

Wedding Guest

By the way, readers, the letter from "Wedding Guest" gives me an opportunity to underscore her flattering remark about the groomsmen. More and more brides and grooms are electing to have their groomsmen wear dark suits. Not only does it save the cost of time and money for rentals, but the man's own suit is likely to fit much better since he would have had it altered especially for him. This is bound to be a plus if you have groomsmen of assorted shapes and sizes. (And who doesn't!)

However, if you do use rented tuxedos, to prevent disaster on the wedding day, please instruct every one, from groom to groomsman, to try on the whole shebang once more *before leaving the store.* Too many guys have discovered that they made the pants too long—twenty minutes before the ceremony began!

Doubt Number Five—"What If the Worst Happens?"

Dear Abby: My wedding plans are all set. The bridesmaids have already bought their dresses and paid for them themselves, but listen to this one: One of my bridesmaids asked me who would reimburse the bridesmaids for the cost of the dresses if I fail to make it to the altar!

Frankly, it never occurred to me that such a thing could happen. It would be a very traumatic happening, but I suppose each bridesmaid would have to handle the loss herself.

Abby, do you think I should have to pay $114 times five?

St. Paul Nightmare

Dear Nightmare: I usually advise people to be prepared for every eventuality, but in this case I say: Don't get the snowplow out until the blizzard hits.

Your Wedding Rings

Choose these together—but the bride shouldn't see hers again until the wedding day. Not so for the groom. Not only does he see it before the wedding, but he and the best man make sure that the wedding ring(s) is in the best man's pocket *before the ceremony*.

If the groom is to receive a ring, the bride pays for it and the best man holds both until the right moment. However, many a groom prefers not to wear a wedding ring, which can lead to a major dispute. Over the years, I have responded to this query often:

Dear Abby: I am getting married soon, but there is one thing we cannot agree on. I want my fiancé to wear a wedding ring after we are married. He says he will not wear one because he does not care for any kind of jewelry.

I told him that he needs to wear a wedding band so women will know that he is a married man. Am I wrong to insist he wear one?

Anonymous Bride

Dear Anonymous: You're being unrealistic. A wedding ring will not stop your husband's circulation—no matter how tight it is. Back off. A wedding band does not a faithful husband make.

In fact, many grooms have a good reason not to wear the ring:

Dear Abby: Recently you published a letter from a bride who was upset because her future husband refused to wear a wedding ring. She feared that no one would know that he was married.

Tell that young woman to fear not. While I was in basic training in Abilene, Texas, in 1944, I didn't want to wear my wedding ring, but my wife insisted on it. Sure enough, while I was helping to stack large cases in very high stacks, I caught my wedding ring on a nail, and nearly tore my finger off! I never wore my wedding ring again.

151

My wife and I will celebrate our fifty-second wedding anniversary soon, so tell "Soon to Wed" she has nothing to worry about.

Larry Taylor
Nashville, Georgia

Settled on rings? You're almost ready—now it's time to decide what to do about "something old, something new, something borrowed, and something blue. . . ."

♥

Wedding Dress Checklist

1. Discuss the kind of wedding you want—formal or informal. Think about the cost to you, your family, and your friends before making your final decision.
2. As soon as possible, select your wedding gown and veil; then choose your attendants' attire. Before you ask anyone to be in your wedding party, be sure to inform them of your plans and the maximum possible cost to them.
3. Make a list of those who agree to be in your wedding party, their addresses and phone numbers, sizes, the outfits, and colors they will wear. Include bridesmaids and groomsmen. Record that information here:

_____

_____

_____

_____

_____

_____

_____

_____

_____

_____

_____

_____

_____

4. Decide who—bride or groom or other person—will stay in touch with whom to be sure all clothing plans are on schedule. Assign one person to be sure rental orders are placed, ready, and—on the day of pick-up—correctly packaged. List who's in charge here:

_____

_____

5. Add a series of dates to your Wedding Countdown on which you will go over the list of participants and clothing to be sure everything is on schedule.
6. Ask one person to be available to help the bride and her bridesmaids on the wedding day with any last-minute alterations or pressing. Ask another person to be available to help the groom and groomsmen.
7. If yours is an informal wedding, ask a close friend to help you in case of any last-minute wardrobe calamities—either yours or another family member's.
8. As early as possible, inform the mother of the bride and the mother of the groom of your wedding plans. Give them the date by which you need to know what they are planning to wear. Add this date to your Wedding Countdown. Ask them if they would like to wear corsages. If so, place the order with the florist.

153

9. Will your honor attendants be dressed differently from the bridesmaids and groomsmen? If so, record the details here. Will you have flower girls or ring-bearers in special outfits? Be sure their names and other information are recorded on your list.

10. As soon as possible, order your rings. Record the pick-up date on your Wedding Countdown.

11. Choose your "Something old, something new . . ." items.

12. One week before the wedding, the bride and groom should each make a complete list of every item—from bridal garb to rings to "going-away" clothes—that should be ready/packed for the wedding.

13. The day before the wedding, the bride and groom should go over the items listed in Number 12—with the maid of honor and best man, respectively—to be sure everything is ready.

14. Record in your Wedding Countdown the dates for your appointments with the hairdresser and the barber.

15. One week before the wedding, confirm "dressing rooms" for bride, groom, bridesmaids, groomsmen, and other members of the wedding party in private homes or at the location of the ceremony.

16. Schedule a weekly review of your "Wedding Dress Checklist" on your Wedding Countdown. Remember, this is likely to involve more people and more details than any other area of your wedding plans.

Don't worry—you'll look wonderful!

Abby

9
Small Kindnesses

Like the budding bloom of a fresh flower, a little thoughtfulness can make a wedding extraordinary for a person too often forgotten.

The physically disabled or mentally disadvantaged friend or relative can pose a special problem for someone working hard to plan a wedding to best accommodate everyone's needs. If you have a question about what is "correct," think last about etiquette—consider only the feelings of the person with special needs. Do what is kind and caring. In my book, *that* qualifies as the "correct" behavior.

Including the Disabled

Do you have an elderly or disabled relative who would treasure your invitation though attending the wedding is out of the question?

If so, but you hesitate for health reasons, use this guideline: Do not send an invitation to someone who is so physically incapacitated that he or she would be not be aware of receiving it, or the need to respond would place a burden on another party.

Do not allow a physical handicap to stand in the way of including people in your wedding party either. Not infrequently I hear from readers who hesitate to include a handicapped person only because they haven't seen it done before and they do not want to embarrass anyone. Here's an example:

155

Dear Abby: My father is in a wheelchair (spinal cord injury) and will never walk again. I am being married and would like to have my father "walk" me down the aisle and give me away in marriage.

Would it look funny if Dad accompanied me down the aisle in his wheelchair? He can operate it himself, so it's not as if I would have to push it. He's not sensitive about being in a wheelchair and says he will do anything I want him to do.

Could I have my older brother walk me down the aisle and have my father waiting for me to give me away in marriage? Could I walk down alone and have my father waiting for me? Please give me some ideas. Thank you.

December Bride

Dear Bride: Any of the options you mentioned is perfectly accept-able. Do whatever is comfortable for you and your father. It's your day. Good luck and God bless.

I repeat: Do whatever is comfortable for you and your handicapped relative or friend. I have heard of marriages where the ceremony was "signed" for family members who were deaf, and other weddings that have been peformed in hospitals and nursing homes.

Just be sure to double-check all the facilities at the location of your ceremony and reception to ensure that the handicapped guest will have easy access. You may want to assign one of your ushers the duty of checking with the guests regularly to prevent any frustrations with parking, getting around, or getting served.

When Death or Illness Become a Factor

On the other hand, illness and death can intrude in other ways that can affect your wedding plans. Please use utmost consideration should you encounter a situation like this bride:

Dear Abby: I am to be married soon and have a very serious problem to face. My fiancé's father is seriously ill. (He's terminal.) The doctors have just given him a period of time to live, which comes very close to our wedding date. We set our wedding date four months ago—before we knew how sick he was.

If he is called by God close to our wedding date, what is the proper etiquette with regard to our wedding? How can we handle the joy of our wedding with the sorrow of his passing, which will be mourned by my fiancé's mother and the rest of his family?

Please answer soon as there isn't much time.

Happy and Sad

Dear Happy and Sad: Should your future father-in-law die on your wedding day, or a few days before, it would cast a sorrowful shadow over the wedding festivities.

Why not change your wedding to an earlier date, so he can have the pleasure of knowing you are married? If this is not possible, then I suggest postponing it until after he answers God's call.

The Hostile Household

Earlier in this chapter and throughout my book, I address problems common to most of us. Sometimes, human nature can be unreasonable, angry, or meanspirited—no matter what efforts are made. We all encounter behavior problems in the people we love from time to time.

Don't let turmoil among your nearest and dearest spoil your wedding plans. Consider the situation and your alternatives, make the decision that works best for the bride and groom and—when in doubt—be kind.

Love,
Abby

Wedding Countdown

(Beside each item, initial who's in charge.)

Check on:	3 Months Prior to Wedding	1 Month	1 Week
Budget			
Ceremony	_____	_____	_____
Reception	_____	_____	_____
Stationery	_____	_____	_____
Clothes	_____	_____	_____
Photos	_____	_____	_____
Flowers	_____	_____	_____
Transportation	_____	_____	_____
Music	_____	_____	_____
Gifts/Rings	_____	_____	_____
Honeymoon	_____	_____	_____
Other	_____	_____	_____
Ceremony			
Clergy	_____	_____	_____
Church or Site	_____	_____	_____
Program (procession, readings, details of ceremony, etc.)	_____	_____	_____

Religious preparation   _____   _____   _____

Legal requirements   _____   _____   _____

Medical requirements   _____   _____   _____

Fees: Set/Paid   _____   _____   _____

Music   _____   _____   _____

Flowers   _____   _____   _____

Other   _____   _____   _____

Bride and Groom

Wedding dress

    Selection order   _____   _____   _____

    Pick-up   _____   _____   _____

    Pressing   _____   _____   _____

    Other ("Something old . . .")   _____   _____   _____

Groom's attire

    Selection order   _____   _____   _____

    Pick-up   _____   _____   _____

    Pressing   _____   _____   _____

    Other (barber, etc.)   _____   _____   _____

Transportation

People   _____   _____   _____

Cars   _____ _____ _____

Maps   _____ _____ _____

Schedule   _____ _____ _____

Fees   _____ _____ _____

Refreshments   _____ _____ _____

Other   _____ _____ _____

Flowers

Ceremony   _____ _____ _____

Reception   _____ _____ _____

Bride   _____ _____ _____

Groom   _____ _____ _____

Wedding party   _____ _____ _____

Aisle runner   _____ _____ _____

"Rice" (or birdseed)   _____ _____ _____

Florist fees   _____ _____ _____

Other   _____ _____ _____

Music

Selections   _____ _____ _____

Musicians   _____ _____ _____

Ceremony   _____ _____ _____

Reception   _____   _____   _____

Schedule   _____   _____   _____

Tapes   _____   _____   _____

Instruments, etc.   _____   _____   _____

Fees   _____   _____   _____

Refreshments   _____   _____   _____

Other   _____   _____   _____

Photos

Photographer   _____   _____   _____

Schedule/List of
desired photos   _____   _____   _____

Cameras/Video equipment   _____   _____   _____

Site requirements checked
(church rules, etc.)   _____   _____   _____

Formal portrait sitting date   _____   _____   _____

Fees   _____   _____   _____

Announcement with photo sent
to local and out-of-town papers   _____   _____   _____

Other   _____   _____   _____

Reception

Site   _____   _____   _____

Caterer or other food
arrangements   _____   _____   _____

Champagne/Liquor/Beverages   _____   _____   _____

Rentals _____ _____ _____

Flowers _____ _____ _____

Music _____ _____ _____

Receiving line plan _____ _____ _____

Cake _____ _____ _____

Dance _____ _____ _____

Toasts _____ _____ _____

Clean-up _____ _____ _____

Schedule of events (toasts,
dancing, cake-cutting, etc.) _____ _____ _____

Fees _____ _____ _____

Other _____ _____ _____

Stationery

Invitations _____ _____ _____

Announcements _____ _____ _____

Ordered _____ _____ _____

Addressed _____ _____ _____

Mailed _____ _____ _____

Thank-yous _____ _____ _____

Fees _____ _____ _____

Responses _____ _____ _____

Wedding invitation list _____ _____ _____

Gift list _____ _____ _____

Other _____ _____ _____

Guests

List _____ _____ _____

Lodging _____ _____ _____

Other _____ _____ _____

Gifts

Register at local stores _____ _____ _____

Thank-yous _____ _____ _____

Display _____ _____ _____

Other _____ _____ _____

Wedding Party

Members _____ _____ _____

Clothing _____ _____ _____

Pick-up _____ _____ _____

Press _____ _____ _____

Lodging _____ _____ _____

Dressing Rooms _____ _____ _____

Transportation _____ _____ _____

Duties (i.e., best man, maid of honor) _____ _____ _____

   Readers _____ _____ _____

   Guest book _____ _____ _____

   Seating charts _____ _____ _____

     Rehearsal dinner _____ _____ _____

     Ceremony _____ _____ _____

     Reception _____ _____ _____

     Parties _____ _____ _____

   Other _____ _____ _____

Honeymoon

   Plan _____ _____ _____

   Tickets _____ _____ _____

   Pack _____ _____ _____

Other

   Prenuptial agreement _____ _____ _____

   Rings _____ _____ _____

     Selected _____ _____ _____

     Picked up _____ _____ _____

   Assistants _____ _____ _____

     Chosen _____ _____ _____

Consulted _____ _____ _____

Lists _____ _____ _____

    Copied _____ _____ _____

    Filed in safe place _____ _____ _____

Final list/Bride and groom _____ _____ _____

    Wedding attire _____ _____ _____

    Going-away clothes _____ _____ _____

    Tickets _____ _____ _____

    Other _____ _____ _____

Bride's List

_____

_____

_____

_____

_____

_____

_____

_____

_____

_____

_____

_____

_____

_____

_____

_____

_____

_____

_____

_____

_____

_____

_____

_____

_____

_____

_____

_____

_____

_____

_____

_____

_____

_____

_____

_____

_____

Groom's List

_____

_____

_____

_____

_____

_____

_____

_____

_____

_____

_____

_____

_____

_____

_____

_____

_____

_____

_____

_____